T0300036

ROUTLEDGE LIBRARY EDITIONS:
ACCOUNTING

Volume 18

MANAGEMENT AUDIT APPROACH IN WRITING BUSINESS HISTORY

MANAGEMENT AUDIT APPROACH IN WRITING BUSINESS HISTORY
A Comparison with Kennedy's Technique on Railroad History

ALLEN L. BURES

Routledge
Taylor & Francis Group

LONDON AND NEW YORK

First published in 1989

This edition first published in 2014
by Routledge
2 Park Square, Milton Park, Abingdon, Oxon, OX14 4RN

and by Routledge
711 Third Avenue, New York, NY 10017

Routledge is an imprint of the Taylor & Francis Group, an informa business

© 1989 Allen L. Bures

British Library Cataloguing in Publication Data
A catalogue record for this book is available from the British Library

ISBN: 978-0-415-53081-1 (Set)
eISBN: 978-1-315-88628-2 (Set)
ISBN: 978-0-415-85421-4 (Volume 18)
eISBN: 978-1-315-88637-4 (Volume 18)

Publisher's Note
The publisher has gone to great lengths to ensure the quality of this reprint but points out that some imperfections in the original copies may be apparent.

Disclaimer
The publisher has made every effort to trace copyright holders and would welcome correspondence from those they have been unable to trace.

Management Audit Approach in Writing Business History

A Comparison with Kennedy's
Technique on Railroad History

Allen L. Bures

Garland Publishing, Inc.
New York & London

Library of Congress Cataloging-in-Publication Data

Bures, Allen L.
Management audit approach in writing business history: a comparison
with Kennedy's technique on railroad history / Allen L. Bures.
p. cm. — (Garland studies in entrepreneurship)
Thesis (Ph. D.)—University of Nebraska, 1980.
Bibliography: p.
ISBN 0-8240-3353-1 (alk. paper)
1. Management audit. 2. Management audit—Case studies.
3. Industrial management—Historiography. 4. Industrial management—
Evaluation—Methodology. 5. Railroads—United States—Management—
Auditing—Case studies. 6. Railroads—United States—Management—
Evaluation—Case studies. 7. Kennedy, Charles Johnston, 1911–
—Chapters on the history of the Boston and Maine Railroad system.
I. Title. II. Series.
HD58.95.B87 1989
338.7'0722—dc20   89-36167

Printed on acid-free, 250-year-life paper

Manufactured in the United States of America

ACKNOWLEDGEMENTS

The author is grateful to those who either directly or indirectly rendered assistance to this study and its completion. First I must express my utmost gratitude for the confidence Dr. Charles J. Kennedy of the University of Nebraska-Lincoln has had in me since I undertook my graduate studies. As my mentor he has helped and supported me whenever the need arose. His insistence on the highest quality of research and writing left an indelible mark. Appreciation is also extended to Dr. Gerald Thompson, Dr. Cary Thorp, Dr. Robert Raymond, and Dr. Phillip McVey for their work as members of my committee.

My wife Simone must be cited for her dedication, patience, understanding, constructive criticism, and moral support; my daughters, Rachelle, and Aysha for surrendering a part of the limited time available with their father; and my parents, Donald and Lois Bures. In ways that only they know, their love and support have made possible the completion of my program of studies.

The author also wishes to acknowledge Isabelle Johnston for her assistance and persistence at the typewriter and patience regardless of the number of alterations and drafts required.

TABLE OF CONTENTS

CHAPTER I

INTRODUCTION

The purpose of this study is to add both to knowledge and method
in the writing of business history. The extent to which the business
historian can credit the role of businessmen (entrepreneurs and managers) to the development of the organization and the economy as a
whole depends in part upon the evaluation of the management ability of
those individuals. That is to say, those businessmen who were only average when they might have been excellent under the same environmental
conditions, certainly could not have made the largest possible contribution.

The degree of management excellence, or lack thereof, in the administration of organizations should be determined in order to establish
the relationship, if any, between management's operation of the organization and the operation of the economy. If one can make that measurement and thereby ascertain the role of an organization's management,
then the business historian is better equipped "to determine how certain
things happened, and thus he will be in a position to write a history
rather than a mere chronicle or description of things that did happen."[1]

[1]Charles J. Kennedy, "Entrepreneurial and Managerial Appraisal in
Writing Railroad History: A Suggestion for a New Approach to Business
History," a paper presented at the Rocky Mountain Social Science
Association, Denver, Colorado, April 28-29, 1972, and printed in the
author's Comments on the History of Business and Capitalism, Especially
in the United States (Lincoln, Nebr.: College of Business Administration, University of Nebraska-Lincoln, 1974), pp. 167-184. The

In this dissertation I put forth the proposition that a workable, adequate, acceptable procedure--a preliminary management audit--can be devised and utilized to gather data, analyze, and compare longitudinally the quality of management existing in organizations. The purpose of this paper is not to make specific assertions about the relationship of various managements to the overall performance of an organization or to the development of the economy, but rather to modify a methodological tool for measuring, analyzing, and comparing managements to aid in the writing of business history.

Professor Charles Kennedy has suggested that when a scholar attempts to evaluate the particular role of entrepreneurs and managers and the effect of their organizations upon society's economic, political, and social development the scholar needs some basis to determine whether the abilities of those individuals were superior, average, or poor considering the conditions under which they had to operate.[2] In a later publication Kennedy developed more fully his classification scheme:

> "Poor" is meant to imply that the net ability was harmful to the future of the company in that certain functions were not performed effectively or were ignored... "Average" is meant to imply that the management of the company was not dangerously weak... "Superior" indicates that the management was definitely above average. The very best of the superior groups could be called "Excellent"....[3]

author has made several small revisions and will use it as the leading essay in his volume entitled Railroad History: Entrepreneurial and Managerial Appraisal and Other Essays, scheduled for publication by EBHA Press in late 1980. The manuscript of his revised version is used throughout this thesis.

[2]Charles J. Kennedy, "Management Appraisal for Historians," presented to a Seminar in Economic and Business History at University of Nebraska-Lincoln, October, 1971.

[3]Kennedy, "Entrepreneurial and Managerial Appraisal ...," p. 1.

Thus, there is a need to construct criteria for excellent management
with illustrations from actual organizations.

The term "preliminary management audit" needs identification and
a comment on what is implied. In essence the preliminary management
audit is a tool--a procedure for systematically examining, analyzing
and appraising a management. It is preliminary in the sense that it is
unrefined and needs further "polishing" to become a final management
audit.[4] A key point is that an appraisal of the management applies to
ability and not mere performance. The relationships posited between
performance, ability, and environmental circumstances may be represented as follows: P = f (A,E), where P (performance) is a f (function) of
A (ability) and E (environmental circumstance).

Consideration of the circumstances and environment under which
management carried out its entrepreneurial and managerial responsibilities is pivotal.[5] Overton has pointed out that advances which seemed
innovating and exciting in their day would in another age look ridicu-
lously crude, or maybe even illegal. In judging events, Overton
asserts that "if one wishes to form a critical opinion of what happened, the basic question to ask is how well any given situation was
met in light of the attendant circumstances."[6]

4Chapter III defines these terms in more detail.

5Chapter II discusses the role of the environment in model building
utilizing the systems approach.

6Richard C. Overton, "Burlington Route: A History of the Burlington
Lines, 1849-1949" (Microfilm copy at University of Nebraska-Lincoln;
master copy at Hagely-Eleutherian Mills Library,Wilmington, Delaware).

An "audit" implies a method of measuring which can produce useful
data. This point is succinctly stated by Professor Emerita Henrietta
Larson of the Harvard Business School in her forward to Charles J.
Kennedy's forthcoming volume of essays which begins with the paper entitled "Entrepreneurial and Managerial Appraisal in Writing Railroad
History: A Suggestion for a New Approach to Business History." Regarding his essays and his unpublished research, Miss Larson refers to
Kennedy's efforts "to design a workable, systematic way of measuring
the demonstrated ability--or lack of it--of a company's executives and
managers, individually and collectively, to deal effectively with their
responsibilities." She adds that his essay on entrepreneurial and managerial appraisal "underscores the often overlooked reality that it is
men rather than institutions that determine the performance of a
company, industry, or business system."[7]

Kennedy states his hypothesis, or, as some historians prefer to
call it, the anticipatory idea, as follows:

1 Management varied between neighboring railroads.
2 Some executives did better than other executives, but if
  one considered the conditions or circumstances, some men,
  managing less prosperous companies, appeared to have
  better ability than the executives of certain companies
  with better performance records.
3 Did not this difference in ability -- or lack thereof --
  make a difference in the history of the company? I.e.,
  circumstances alone did not account for all of the
  differences.
4 The result made a difference in the role of the railroad -- its service to shippers, travelers, employees,
  stockholders, and the public generally.[8]

---

[7]Quoted in Charles J. Kennedy, A New Approach to the History of the
American Business System (Lincoln: University of Nebraska, 1979), p.4.

[8] Ibid., p. 7.

Kennedy's "Management Appraisal" is a more refined and developed technique than the preliminary management audit proposed here. Nevertheless, the preliminary management audit refined and developed, can become an extremely valuable tool for the business historian, and is thus a purposeful academic endeavor. Although this briefer method is not adequate for writing a complete history, it is a tool most useful for the initial analysis.

Some norm of what constitutes the various categories of management excellence is essential to both a management appraisal and a preliminary management audit. These categories could be established in a variety of different ways, one of which would be to study a large number of organizations in detail to determine comparatively what emerges as excellence. Another approach, however, is to study a sampling of organizations in a particular industry over a period of time.

As a beginning contribution to the research needed, this study attempts to establish tentative criteria and examples of excellent management from a sample of the nation's first large-scale organization--the railroads. The railroad industry is attractive for this purpose because (1) of Kennedy's research in the use of management appraisal of early railroads[9] and (2) because prior to the 1870s it was the only big business in the United States. Peter Drucker feels the early railroads emerged as a managerial problem which made obsolescent

---

[9]Chapter IV discusses Kennedy's research in greater detail.

traditional structures and concepts and required effective management.[10] Kennedy has distilled from his research and review of the
literature six significant roles of the railroads, namely,

> 1. The railroads stimulated the development of cities, large
> and small, in all sections of the country. ...
> 2. Railroads made possible the rapid settlement of the West. ...
> 3. Railroads expanded the market areas, thus (a) making
> possible the rapid economic development of large sections of
> the country, (b) encouraging territorial specialization, and
> (c) facilitating specialization within the factory by economies
> of scale derived from larger markets.
> 4. Railroads aided the development of manufacturing (a) by
> providing orders for construction and maintenance, and (b) by
> providing lower transportation costs and inventory costs which
> reduced the total costs of production.
> 5. Railroads were the first big business in the United States,
> and throughout the 1800s devised new techniques in management
> and contributed to the development of the modern corporation.
> 6. Railroads raised the level of living by (a) lowering real
> prices for transportation and (b) by stimulating industriali-
> zation and universal productivity.[11]

North concurs and in addition credits the railroads with substantial

effects upon management development. He points out that not only were

the railroads the first billion-dollar industry, but because of their

size, they required the development of sophisticated methods of large-

scale business organization. Moreover, the needs of these growing,

thriving enterprises required huge amounts of raw materials, and thus

required the expansion of other industries as well.[12] As a result of

---

[10]Peter F. Drucker, An Introductory View of Management (New York:
Harper & Row, 1977), p. 24.

[11]Charles J. Kennedy, Roots of the American Business System: An Introduction to Further Reading and Oral Lectures (Lincoln: College of
Business Administration, University of Nebraska-Lincoln, 1978),
pp. 136-137.

[12]Douglas C. North, Growth and Welfare in the American Past (Englewood
Cliffs, New Jersey: Prentice-Hall, 1966), p. 108.

the railroads, new administrative challenges evolved unprecedented in American business. An elucidating example is provided by taking note of the various segments of Alfred Chandler's book, The Railroads: The Nation's First Big Business, namely, the railroads as promoters of economic change, the beginnings of modern corporate finance, the first modern corporate management, the beginnings of modern labor relations, new ways of competition, and the beginnings of modern governmental regulation of business.[13] This same attitude toward the significance of the railroads prevails in Chandler's 1978 Pulitzer prize winner, The Visible Hand: The Managerial Revolution in American Business.[14] Thus, the railroads are a logical starting place for the development of appropriate tools for the evaluation of the specific role of management in business.

In this study, the preliminary management audit technique is tested as a methodological tool to help explain the role of management excellence within given environmental conditions. The major thrust of this study is two-fold and will center around the following two questions:

1. Are the findings of a preliminary management audit for the years 1870, 1880, 1890, and 1900 for five selected railroads compatible with Kennedy's findings from a complete management appraisal of fifteen major railroads in North Central New England?

---

[13]Alfred D. Chandler, Jr., The Railroads: The Nation's First Big Business (New York: Harcourt, Brace and World, 1965).

[14]Alfred D. Chandler, Jr., The Visible Hand: The Managerial Revolution In American Business (Cambridge: Harvard University Press, 1977).

2. How useful is the preliminary management audit technique
   in writing business history?

Several research procedures have been utilized to answer these two
central questions:

1. Data was collected chronologically (1870, 1880, 1890, and
   1900) for the following railroads: Atchison, Topeka, and
   Santa Fe Railroad Company; Boston and Maine Railroad Company;
   Chicago, Burlington, and Quincy Railroad Company; Illinois
   Central Railroad Company and the Louisville and Nashville
   Railroad Company. The selection of the five roads was based
   upon availability of data, cross-sectionality, and possibili-
   ties of comparison.

2. A preliminary audit of the five railroads for 1870, 1880,
   1890, and 1900 was conducted, utilizing the "Management
   Appraisal Guide for American Railroads," an analytical tool
   especially designed by Charles Kennedy.[15]

In this paper the completed preliminary management audits are compared with Kennedy's findings from fifteen North Central New England
railroads. Finally, the usefulness of the preliminary management audit
as a method of writing business history is discussed.

Because there is a great need for research concerning organizations and management, this study concerns itself with both descriptive
findings and normative considerations. Major changes in most fields

---

[15]Appendix A includes the questionnaire utilized.

occur with the development of new conceptual schemes or paradigms. The study of history requires diverse approaches, and for each of these there is not a single appropriate method but suitable methods which need to be discovered and explored.[16] As Hugh G. J. Aitken notes, the "real challenge is . . . not that of mastering existing approaches but that of developing new ones."[17] This study then poses the preliminary management audit as a new paradigm for appraising management in terms of business history.

_____

[16]George Rogers Taylor, Introduction to Approaches to American Economic History (Charlottesville: University Press of Virginia, 1971), p. vii.

[17]Hugh G. J. Aitken, "The Entrepreneurial Approach to Economic History," in George R. Taylor and L. F. Ellsworth, eds., Approaches to American Economic History (Charlottesville:University Press of Virginia, 1971), p. 1.

CHAPTER II

BUSINESS HISTORY, MODELS, AND THEORY

Since this study concerns itself with business history it seems
reasonable to propose a brief explanation of what is meant by the term
"business history" and the role that theory and models play in the writing of business history. Robertson argues that "business history is
simply a specialty, focusing on the behavior of the firm and its management, within the larger field of economic history."[1] However,
Krooss and Gilbert expand on the field of inquiry and conclude by
stating that, "The history of business is the story of how the business
system and the businessman came to be what they are today."[2] For the
purposes of this study, then, business history is recognized as focusing on the obstacles, problems, issues and opportunities that managers
have faced, the solutions they tried, their related successes and failures, the organizations they built, and the relationships between them.

As was noted earlier, the purpose of this work is to provide a
tool for analyzing and measuring the contribution that business in general and management in particular have played in American history and
as an aid in writing business history. Many people have formed their

[1]Ross M. Robertson, History of the American Economy, 3rd. ed. (New
York: Harcourt Brace Jovanovich, 1973), p. 15.

[2]Herman E. Krooss and Charles Gilbert, American Business History
(Englewood Cliffs, New Jersey: Prentice-Hall, 1972), p. 1.

opinions concerning the nature of this contribution on the basis of inadequate or biased historical writing, for the writing of business
history is heir to the same pitfalls as the writing of any other kind of
history. A balance in both depth and distance is extremely important.
The stream of history is something more than the muck on the bottom or
the froth on the surface.[3] And, as Carl Sagan, writing about another
field of inquiry notes:

> There are many instances . . . where those closest to the in-
> tricacies of the subject have a more highly developed (and
> ultimately erroneous) sense of its intractability than those
> at some remove. On the other hand, those at too great a
> distance may, I am well aware, mistake ignorance for
> perspective.[4]

It is hoped that the tool presented in this paper will help business
historians avoid this pitfall by placing management in the context of
the environmental setting of the times.

As for the inadequacies of extant historical accounts regarding
the role of business, many contemporary American historians feel that
"revision is needed in existing interpretations to show realistically
the role of business in American development."[5] Professor Emeritus
Allan Nevins of Columbia also belongs to this group of "revisionists."
In reviewing Nevins' beliefs, Walton notes that "One charge he makes
is that many historians have neglected business; the other, perhaps
more serious, is that some have misinterpreted the facts through

---

[3]See, for example, Scott D. Walton, _Business In American History_
(Columbus, Ohio: Grid, 1971), p. 10.

[4]Carl Sagan, _The Dragons of Eden_ (New York: Ballantine Books, 1977),
p. 7.

[5]Walton, p. 10.

conscious or unconscious bias" and that "historical writing is a blend of facts and interpretations."[6]

The writing of business history, like the writing of any kind of history, is exceedingly challenging. Managers of complex organizations make decisions which have tremendous impacts. The task of describing this system of interaction in all its intricate detail seems difficult and extremely time consuming. The business historian is confronted with a jumble of facts that he must collect and transform into an intelligible, significant narrative.[7]

At this point, the job of the business historian is very much like that of the organization and management theorist--he must abstract from the r: of the specific in order to see the fundamental forces at work. Insofar as he abstracts from reality in order to discover principles, he is a theorist.[8]

The role of theory is pivotal in the examination of historical data. Robertson's remarks on pages ten and eleven of his textbook are stated exceptionally well. He concludes that "whether we like it or not, history involves implicit theorizing."[9]

---

[6]Walton, p. 10.

[7]Robertson, p. 10.

[8]We commonly hear the expression "That's all right in theory, but it won't work in practice." This statement, if it makes sense at all means "If we grant your assumptions, what you say is true, but your assumptions are so far from reality that your analysis could never be of use in solving a real problem." If a theory is not right in practice, then the theory is wrong.

[9]Robertson, p. 11.

A caveat, however, should be given against expecting too much of business history as a testing ground for theorms; for it is sometimes next to impossible to isolate only the relevant historical variables to the satisfaction of other historians. Yet, a careful and judicious observation of repeated phenomena may give us some confidence to verify or refute propositions reached by abstract reasoning. It is in this context that business history can offer its most valuable insights.

The object of business history, then, or any historical inquiry for that matter, should not be simply to reproduce or to reconstruct, but to understand. Peterson, writing about one of the sister social sciences, economics, notes:

> The world of reality is a complex of forces so vast that no one
> could possibly comprehend all their relationships. If progress
> is to be made toward understanding reality, it is essential to
> simplify the complexities of the real world. We can do this by
> directing our investigation toward the forces or factors be-
> lieved to be of strategic importance for an understanding of
> how things do work in the real world.[10]

Of particular importance is the process of abstraction to enable "understanding" and explanatory power. As Luthans states, "The purpose of any theory is understanding, prediction, and control. When theories become perfected, they should have general application."[11] Moreover, as Lewin aptly states, "Nothing is quite so practical as a good theory."[12]

---

[10]Wallace C. Peterson, Income, Employment, and Economic Growth(New York: W. W. Norton, 1967), p. 12.

[11]Fred Luthans, Introduction to Management: A Contingency Approach (New York: McGraw Hill, 1976), p. 238.

[12]Kurt Lewin, "Group Decisions and Social Changes," in Readings in Social Psychology, eds. T. Newcomb and E. Hartley (New York: Holt, Rhinehart and Winston, 1947), p. 24.

One of the tools most useful to the theorist is a model or conceptual framework. The model should not be viewed as a detailed and photographically faithful reproduction in miniature, but rather as a simplified portrait whose purpose is to make the organization, its variables, and their relationships more intelligible. The emphasis here is on intelligibility without oversimplification. For the more complicated and realistic a model, the more unwieldy it becomes a tool for analysis. Tersine and Jones comment that a "conceptual model becomes useful when it assists in making order out of confusing data. Its value lies in allowing experimental pretesting of decisions." Furthermore, "a model is neither true nor false; the standard for comparing models is utility, i.e., adequate description or successful prediction."[13]

The "usefulness" of a model lies in its power to disclose and to enable understanding and explanation. On a conceptual level, understanding is the power to render experience intelligible by bringing perceived particulars under appropriate concepts. Further, understanding must involve classifying variables and noting uniformities and/or interrelationships between them. According to Clark, in theory and in practice it is sensible to view any organization as a configuration of interacting variables, some of which are more highly interdependent than others.[14] Thus, useful models must include meaningful

[13]R. J. Tersine and M. B. Jones, "Models for Examining Organizations," Journal of Systems Management, 24, No. 9 (1973), p. 33.

[14]P. A. Clark, Action Research and Organizational Change (New York: Harper & Row, 1965), p. 2-3.

generalizations pertaining to relationships between variables.

The business historian, because he is also a theorist whose task is to analyze complex organizations, must construct a useful model or set of models for his purposes. It is here that the subject of this paper comes into focus, for what is proposed is a conceptual model for analyzing and appraising management. Such a conceptual model, here-after referred to as the preliminary management audit has great poten-tial usefulness for the business historian. Kennedy points out how im-portant is the task of evaluating management, and how cumbersome this task can be without a model. Without such models, "It will be necessary to identify a number of firms ... which appear to have the best records in a specific function or aspect of management during a particular period of history, so that those firms or non-profit units can be used tentatively as 'measuring sticks.' "[15] Consequently, there exists a real need for the model that is proposed here.

In order for a model to be useful in this complex area of manage-ment appraisal, it must, as Jackson Martindell notes, meet certain requirements.[16]

1. It must be flexible: applicable to managements of all kinds in all fields of endeavor.

2. It must be comprehensive: it must ensure that the analyst will know what questions must be asked in order to obtain a clear picture of the enterprise he is studying.

---

[15]Kennedy, 'Management Appraisal for Historians."

[16]Jackson Martindell, The Appraisal of Management: For Executives and and Investors, rev. ed. (New York: Harper & Row, 1965), pp. 2-3.

3. It must permit comparison between managements: so it must
   ask the same questions in the same form in order that one
   enterprise's answer may be placed against another's.

4. It must supply measuring sticks of the quality of management,
   reflected in the answers to its questions.

5. It must consider the interrelation of all management functions.

However, no matter what framework is devised for analysis, there
is one other crucial factor that must be kept in mind; the fact that
one part of the management process affects and is affected by all the
others.[17] The methodology for understanding management and organizational behavior must, then, take a "systems" approach. It should be
pointed out here that those individuals who struggled to establish what
later became known as "systems theory" were primarily concerned with a
methodological problem, that of finding the most appropriate method of
studying any complex entity or system. The traditional analytical
method of investigation is a piece-meal one in the sense that an entity
is divided into simple component parts which are investigated separately. Systems theorists maintain that this is inappropriate for understanding "wholes" or "organized complexities" or "systems." The pecul-
iarity which these "systems" possess, they argue, is that they have
parts which cannot be meaningfully separated from each other.[18]

---

[17]Ibid., p. 2-3.

[18]For useful treatises concerning system modeling see for example:
Kenneth Boulding, "General Systems Theory: The Skeleton of Science,"
Management Science, April 1956, pp. 197-208; Daniel Katz and Robert
L. Kahn, The Social Psychology of Organizations (New York: John Wiley

Indeed, it can be seen that the parts of any analysis do not exist in isolation. When analyzing history, this is particularly true. Angyal notes that

> ...When the single objects a, b, c, d, are based together in an aggregate they participate in that aggregation as object a, object b, object c, etc., that is, as lines, distances, color spots, or whatever they may be. When, however, a whole is constituted by the utilization of objects a, b, c, d, the parts of the resulting whole are not object a, object b, object, etc., but α, β, γ, δ ... .[19]

Thus, if part α is moved from the system or whole for examination in isolation, it is no longer α, for it is no longer related to the other parts; the act of removing α changes it, and it becomes artifact A.

The general theme of the systems approach, therefore, is that all phenomena, whether in the universe at large or in an organizational setting, are related in some way.

Since all management functions affect each other, the systems approach is the method most appropriate to the study of management. Moreover, it is the comprehensive "open" system that provides an excellent conceptual paradigm. As explained by Katz and Kahn,

> Traditional organization theories have tended to view the human organization as a closed system. This view tendency has led to a disregard of differing organizational environments and the nature of organizational dependency on environment.[20]

---

and Sons, 1966); J. D. Thompson, Organizations In Action (New York: McGraw-Hill, 1967); J. P. Van Gigch, Applied General Systems Theory, (New York: Harper & Row, 1974).

[19]A. Angyal, "A Logic of Systems," in Systems Thinking, ed. F. E. Emery (Baltimore, MD: Penguin Books, 1962), p. 168.

[20]Katz & Kahn, p. 29.

This contrast is illustrated in Figures 2:1 and 2:2. Figure 2:1 depicts the traditional closed model, and Figure 2:3, a simple open system.

Figure 2:1 - A Traditional Closed System Model

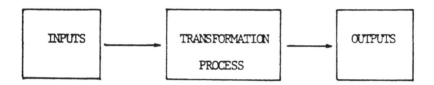

Figure 2:2 - A Simple Open System Model

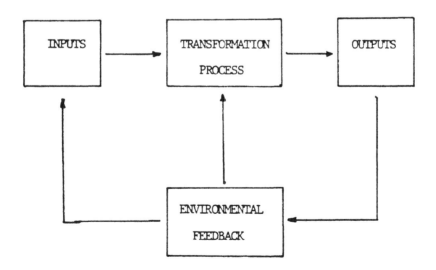

However, Figure 2:3, a more complex open system model, more realistically represents the organization and its management as an exchange
with the environment. Notice that porosity and permeability character-
ize the organization's boundary.

Figure 2:3 - A More Complex Open System

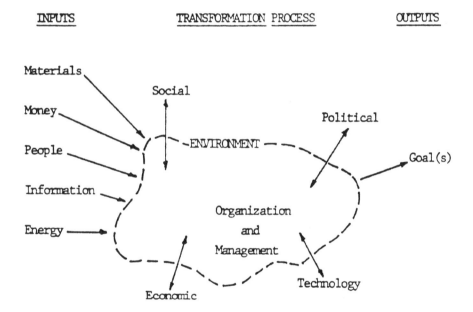

All organizations are open to environmental influences, although
obviously some are more open than others. One difficulty inherent in
studying the relationship of an organization to its environment is that
the organization must be distinguished from its environment. This is
not easy to do, however, The boundary between organization and environment is partially an arbitrary invention of the perceiver.

In a revealing analogy, Starbuck compares the organization to a cloud or magnetic field. He points out that when one is emersed within it, the characteristics are quite obvious. So also when one is looking on from a distance. But as one approaches the boundary, "the boundary fades into ambiguity and becomes only a region of gradual transition..." Like the organization, "one can sometimes say 'Now I am inside' or 'Now I am outside,' but he can never confidently say 'This is the boundary.' "21

Thus, the open system theory will be utilized along with the conceptual framework of a preliminary management audit to provide a new paradigm for the writing of business history. Like all new paradigms it may at first seem somewhat crude and imprecise. As Kast and Rosenzweig remark, new paradigms

> ...do not display the clarity and certainty of older paradigms that have been refined through years of research and writing. But a new paradigm does provide for a new start and opens up new directions that were not possible under the old.22

In addition, as Kuhn warns us, a new paradigm may appear at first to be "very limited in both scope and precision." He adds that a paradigm gains status when it is more successful than its competitors "in solving a few problems that the group of practitioners has come to realize as acute," even though it is not "completely successful with a

---

21W. H. Starbuck,"Organizations and Their Environments" in Handbook of Industrial and Organizational Psychology, ed. M. D. Dunnette (Chicago: Rand McNally, 1976), p. 1071.

22Fremont E. Kast and James Rosenzweig, Organization and Management (New York: McGraw-Hill, 1979), p. 17.

single problem or notably successful with any large number."[23] The
author hopes that this new paradigm will add significantly to the study
of management and organizations in the business history area of scholar-
ly inquiry.

---

[23]Thomas S. Kuhn, The Structure of Scientific Revolutions (Chicago:
University of Chicago Press, 1962), p. 23.

CHAPTER III

THE MANAGEMENT AUDIT CONCEPT

Business history and the role of theory and models in the writing
of business history were discussed in Chapter II. The concept of a
preliminary management audit using a comprehensive open systems
approach was proposed as a valuable tool for the writing of business
history. Before elaborating further on the nature of this tool, the
meaning of "management" and "auditing," as well as the concept of the
"management audit" itself should be clarified.

MANAGEMENT

Management has been popularly defined as "getting things done
through people."[1] According to Kast and Rosenzweig, management "involves the coordination of human and material resources toward objective accomplishment,"[2] or, as Martindell notes, "the art of bringing
ends and means together, the art of purposeful action."[3] Typical definitions suggest that management is a process of planning, organizing and
controlling activities. Some definitions increase the number of sub-

[1]Richard M. Hodgetts, Management: Theory, Process, and Practice
(Philadelphia: W. B. Saunders, 1979), p. 5.

[2]Fremont E. Kast and James Rosenzweig, Organization and Management
(New York: McGraw-Hill, 1979), p. 17.

[3]Jackson Martindell, The Appraisal of Management: For Executives and
Investors, rev. ed. (New York: Harper and Row, 1965), p. xiii.

processes to include activating and motivating; other definitions reduce the scheme to include only planning and implementation. See Table 3:1. For the purposes of this study, management will be defined as the coordination of resources toward goal accomplishment. Four basic elements of this definition can be isolated. Thus, management functions (1) toward goal accomplishment, (2) through other people, (3) via various techniques, and (4) in an organizational setting. This definition is based upon the assumption that the need for management arises whenever work is specialized and undertaken by two or more persons.[4]

The study of management is relatively new in our society, although it has a long history.[5] One of the earliest accounts which considers management as an important factor is Alexander Hamilton's famous "Report on Manufactures" written in the late 18th century.[6] He emphasized the constructive, purposeful and systematic role of management and the organization. In fact, he viewed management, rather than economic forces, as the "engine" of economic and social development, and organization as the "carrier" of economic advance.[7]

Robert Owen, a plant owner in New Lenark, Scotland in the early

---

[4]This idea is essentially the one developed in James D. Mooney, The Principles of Organization (New York: Harper & Brothers, 1947).

[5]See especially Anthony Tillett, Thomas Kempner and Gordon Wills, Management Thinkers (Baltimore, MD: Penguin Books, 1970); Claude S. George, Jr., The History of Management Thought, 2nd ed. (Englewood Cliffs, N.J.: Prentice-Hall, 1972);Daniel A. Wren, The Evolution of Management Thought (New York: Ronald Press, 1972).

[6]Peter F. Drucker, An Introductory View of Management, (New York: Harper and Row, 1977), p. 23.

[7]Ibid.

TABLE 3:1

The Management Process as Seen by Various Authors

Functions	Fayol	Haimann & Scott	Koontz & O'Donnell	Sisk	Wren & Voich
Planning	X	X	X	X	X
Organizing	X	X	X	X	X
Commanding	X				
Staffing		X	X		
Directing			X		
Influencing		X			
Coordinating	X				
Leading				X	
Controlling	X	X	X	X	X

Sources: Henri Fayol, Industrial and General Management, trans. by J. A. Coubrough (London: Sir Isaac Pitman and Sons, 1949); Theo Haimann, William Scott, and Patrick E. Connor, Managing the Modern Organization, 3rd edition (Boston: Houghton Mifflin, 1978); Harold Koontz and Cyril O'Donnell, Management: A Systems and Contingency Analysis of Managerial Functions, 6th edition (New York: McGraw-Hill, 1976); Henry L. Sisk, Management and Organization, 3rd edition (Chicago: South-Western, 1977); Daniel A. Wren and Dan Voich, Jr., Principles of Management: Process and Behavior, 2nd edition (New York: The Ronald Press, 1976).

1800s was one of the first to tackle the problem of productivity and motivation, or the relationships between the worker and his fellow worker, the organization and management. With Owen, the manager emerges as a real person. But, as Drucker notes, "it was a long time before Owen had successors."[8]

It was only with the advent of complex business structures and other large-scale organizations that management emerged as an important social factor. In fact, the railroads, as one of the earliest complex business enterprises, contributed significantly to the growth of management. As Chandler notes in his work, The Railroads: The Nation's First Big Business, the size and complexity of railroad operations required new methods and new forms. He points out that

> ...The railroads were the first American business to work out the modern ways of finance, management, labor relations, competition and government regulation. Railroad promoters and managers pioneered in all these areas ...because they had to.[9]

Since its emergence as an important social form, management has flourished. Peter Drucker points out that

> The emergence of management ... is a pivotal event in social history....Rarely in human history has a new institution proven indispensable so quickly....Management which is ... specifically charged ... with the responsibility for organized economic advance, therefore reflects the basic spirit of the modern age. It is in fact indispensable--and this explains why, once begotten it grew so fast and with so little opposition.[10]

---

[8]Ibid., p. 24.

[9]Alfred D. Chandler, Jr., The Railroads: The Nation's First Big Business (New York: Harcourt, Brace & World, 1965), p. 9.

[10]Peter F. Drucker, The Practice of Management (New York: Harper and Row, 1950), pp. 3-4.

The field of management as an area of study has generated a relatively large volume of literature in a short period of time. Compared with other academic disciplines, the study of modern management is very young.[11] Nevertheless, management has a rich heritage and some would argue that it "has been in the forefront of what progress society has made through the years."[12]

AUDITING

The word "audit" usually brings to mind a public accounting firm. In fact, however, there are three different kinds of audits: the external audit, the internal audit, and the management audit.[13] Auditing, then, may be defined along several lines, depending upon the purpose to be served.

The American Accounting Association Committee on Basic Auditing Concepts has prepared the following comprehensive definition of auditing.

> Auditing is a systematic process of objectively obtaining and evaluating evidence regarding assertions about economic actions and events to ascertain the degree of correspondence between those assertions and established criteria and communicating the results to interested users.[14]

---

[11]Sidney Pollard, The Genesis of Modern Management, A Study of the Industrial Revolution In Great Britain (Cambridge: Harvard University Press, 1965).

[12]Fred Luthans, Introduction to Management: A Contingency Approach (New York: McGraw-Hill, 1976), p. 3.

[13]Hodgetts, p. 150.

[14]American Accounting Association Committee on Auditing Concepts, "A Statement of Basic Auditing Concepts," Accounting Review, supplement to Vol. 47, 1972.

This definition is broad and general enough to encompass most auditing activity. Specific kinds of auditing, however, require more specific definitions.

An external audit is conducted by outside accounting personnel and entails the examination and evaluation of the firm's financial transactions and accounts. The American Institute of Certified Public Accountants (AICPA) describes the principal objectives of an external audit as follows:

> The objective of the ordinary examination of financial state-
> ments by the independent auditor is the expression of an
> opinion on the fairness with which they present financial
> position, results of operations and changes in financial
> position in conformity with generally accepted accounting
> principles. The auditor's report is the medium through which
> he expresses his opinion or, if circumstances require, dis-
> claims an opinion. In either case, he states whether his
> examination has been made in accordance with generally
> accepted auditing standards.[15]

Usually this audit entails a detailed verification of traditional financial statements for the purpose of rendering a standard audit report. The external audit does not delve into non-financial areas such as evaluating policy, plans, and procedures.

An internal audit is conducted by the organization's own staff specialists. Internal auditing in its early days was largely a clerical activity which concerned itself with the detection and prevention

---

[15]AICPA Statement on Auditing Standards No. 1 1973. Statements On Auditing Procedures Numbers 1 - 54 were codified into SAS No. 1. In 1973; and Statements on Auditing Standards numbered 2 through 22 had been issued by March 1978.

of clerical errors and fraud.[16] While today the internal auditor still
performs these functions, his work is of a much broader scope as the
following Institute of Internal Auditors' (IIA) statement indicates:

> The objective of internal auditing is to assist members of
> the organization in the effective discharge of their responsi-
> bilities. To this end, internal auditing furnishes them with
> analyses, appraisals, recommendations, counsel, and information
> concerning the activities reviewed.[17]

Although much of the internal auditor's effort is restricted to
financial areas, sometimes he goes further and approaches what is
commonly known as the management audit.[18]

MANAGEMENT AUDITING

The audit of management[19] (as opposed to reviews for management)
has received increasing attention in recent years.[20] Interest comes

---

[16]Rufus Wixon, ed., Accountants' Handbook (New York: Ronald Press,
1965), p. 1.5.

[17]The Institute of Internal Auditors, Inc., Standards for the Professional Practice of Internal Auditing, 1978.

[18]Hodgetts, p. 151.

[19]"Operational audit," "Functional audit," "management audit,"
"management appraisal," "audit of management," and "systems audit,"
are terms often used.

[20]See especially American Institute of Management, Appraising a Manage-
ment, 1, No. 21 (1950); American Institute of Management, The Manage-
ment Audit Bookshelf, 12 vols. (New York: American Institute of
Management, 1959); Association of Consulting Management Engineers,
ACME Reporter, 1, No. 4 (June 1, 1950); Bruce W. Beloit, "Appraisal
of Management Competence As A Measurement in Economic and Business
History Research" (Unpublished Master's Thesis, University of
Nebraska, 1967); Mary C. Bromage, "Wording the Management Audit,"
The Journal of Accountancy, Feb. 1972, pp. 50-57; Robert B. Buchele,
"How to Evaluate A Firm," Californian Management Review, Fall 1962,
pp. 5-17; John C. Burton, "Management Auditing," The Journal of

from several sources. Investment analysts recognize that the evaluation of management is of crucial importance. Similarly, stockholders may want more assurance that their capital is being used effectively. In addition, there is an increasing tendency on the part of the public to feel that a firm's management has a responsibility to use resources as a service to society as well as to benefit its stockholders. In

---

Accountancy, May 1968, pp. 41-46; M. A. Cayley, "Marketing-Research Planning and Evaluation," The Business Quarterly, 40, No. 1 (Spring 1975), pp. 30-36; George T. Conly, "Happiness is a Management Audit," The Journal of Accountancy, March 1973, pp. 89-90; Frank DeWitt, "Measuring Management Performance," Management Accounting,Nov. 1972, pp. 18-22; Denny Drombrower, "The Professional Accountants Formula for Survival, Operational Auditing," Canadian Chartered Accountant 101, No. 6 (Dec. 1972), p. 53; John A. Edds, Auditing for Management (Toronto: Sir Isaac Pitman, 1971); Frank Gentile, "Statistical Sampling--The Auditor's Best Friend," International Journal of Government Auditing, 1, No. 2 (April 1974), pp. 2-3, 16; William J. Gravelle, "How to Conduct an Operational Audit," Bank Administration, 50, No. 9 (Sept. 1974), pp. 76-80; Henry H. Guck, "The Psychology of Management Audits," Management Accounting, 56, No. 3 (Sept. 1974),pp. 41-44; William T. Greenwood, Business Policy: A Management Audit Approach (New York: Macmillan, 1967); John H. Kelly, "Productivity is Something that Should be Audited," The Office, 79, No. 1 (Jan. 1974),p. 98; Charles J. Kennedy, "Commuter Services in the Boston Area, 1835-1860," read at joint session of American Historical Association and the Lexington Group, Dec. 30, 1960, and printed in The Business History Review, 36 (1962), pp. 153-170; Charles J. Kennedy, Management Apprai- sal for Historians (Lincoln: College of Business Administration, University of Nebraska-Lincoln, 1971); Charles J. Kennedy, "Entrepre- neurial and Managerial Appraisal in Writing Railroad History: A Suggestion for a New Approach to Business History," read at Rocky Mountain Social Science Association, April 22, 1972, and printed in the author's Comments on the History of Business and Capitalism, Especially in the United States (Lincoln: College of Business Administration, University of Nebraska-Lincoln, 1974), pp. 167-184, and to be reprinted with a slight revision in the author's forthcoming volume, Railroad History: Entrepreneurial and Managerial Appraisal and Other Essays (EBHA Press); Charles J. Kennedy, "Top Management of American Railroads, 1830-1870," read at the Western Social Science Association, May 1, 1975, and to be printed in the author's forthcoming Railroad History ... Essays; Charles J. Kennedy, Railroad Management to 1870: The Predecessors of the Boston and Maine System (planned for publication in 1981); Lennis M. Knighton, "Information Preconditions of Performance Auditing," Governmental Finance, 5, No. 2 (May 1976), pp. 22-27;

essence, concern is expressed not only with "financial results but also to the effectiveness of management's stewardship."[21]

The management audit concept has been variously defined. One of the first to write of the management audit concept was Henri Fayol in the early 1900s.[22] He suggested a periodic "management audit" using summarized charts.[23] Neal, in the 1950s, utilized management audit data of the American Institute of Management to analyze the excellence of management in New England.[24] The American Institute of Management is generally considered the grandfather of the management audit, pro-

---

William P. Leonard, The Management Audit (Englewood Cliffs: Prentice-Hall, 1962); Lloyd K. Marquis, "A Comprehensive Framework for Analyzing the Management of a Business Enterprise," in Papers of the Sixteenth Business History Conference, Charles Kennedy, ed. (Lincoln: College of Business Administration, University of Nebraska-Lincoln, 1969), pp. 38-48; Jackson Martindell, The Appraisal of Management: For Executives and Investors, rev. ed. (New York: Harper & Row, 1965); Desmond B. J. Morin, "The Operational Audit," International Journal of Government Auditing, 1, No. 1 (Jan. 1974), pp. 2-3; Lawrence M. Murray, "Management Audit of Divisional Performance," Management Accounting, 54, No. 9 (March 1973), pp. 26-28; Charles H. Smith, Roy A. Lanier, and Martin Taylor, "The Need and Scope of the Audit of Management: A Survey of Attitudes," Accounting Review, 47 (April 1972), pp. 270-283; Olin C. Snellgrove, "The Management Audit-- Organizational Guidance System," Journal of Systems Management, 22, No. 12 (Dec. 1971), p. 10; Allen Weiss, "Management Audits--The Development of a New Service," LKHH Accountant, 63, No. 3 (Autumn 1973), pp. 46-49.

[21]Burton, p. 41.

[22]Fayol, p. 77.

[23]Tillet et al., p. 117.

[24]Alfred C. Neal, "New England's Industrial Management," in The Economic State of New England, eds., Arthur A. Bright, Jr. and George H. Ellis (New Haven: Yale University Press, 1954), pp. 527-555.

posing it as "a procedure for systematically examining, analyzing, and appraising a management's overall performance"[25] to determine if a company qualifies for the Institute's rating of "excellent." No attempt has been made by the Institute in its published studies to rate companies as average, mediocre, or poor.

Leonard, in a major treatise dealing with most aspects of management audit, uses the following definition:

> The management audit is . . . a comprehensive and constructive examination of an organizational structure of a company, institution, or branch of government, or any component thereof, such as a division or department, and its use of human and physical facilities.[26]

Like the American Institute of Management, Leonard affirms that a management audit must examine and appraise the performance from the point of view of the "whole." With a similar view Greenwood notes that an audit of the overall organization essentially may be defined as a measurement and evaluation of total organizational performance.[27]

Thus, a management audit is concerned with systematically examining, analyzing, and appraising a management's overall performance and not only the financial results.[28] This thinking led Hodgetts to comment that "a management audit picks up where a financial audit

---

[25]Martindell, p. 48. The AIM in fact registered the term "The Management Audit." However, as William T. Greenwood, in Business Policy: A Management Audit Approach (New York: Macmillan, 1967), p. 48, notes, "Nevertheless, the term has become generic."

[26]William P. Leonard, The Management Audit (Englewood Cliffs: Prentice-Hall, 1962), p. 35.

[27]Greenwood, p. 4.

[28]Burton, p. 41.

leaves off."[29] Buchele develops this point with the statement that
"Shrewd analysts today must not only x-ray its management and marketing
potential, but also its vulnerability to future shifts in technology."[30] Sawyer further contrasts financial auditing with management
auditing. He notes that

> Financial auditing...is concerned primarily with the verification
> of financial statements....It restricts itself to accounting
> controls, /and/ is concerned essentially with historical,
> financial data..../Management/ auditing...is concerned with
> operating /administrative/controls /and/...may be applied to
> all parts of an enterprise. /Management auditing/ interprets
> and uses operating as well as financial data, /including/...
> historical data as a means of finding ways of improving future
> business operations.[31]

Consequently, the primary objective of a management audit is to reveal
strengths, weaknesses, irregularities, shortcoming and the like--
actual and potential--which can aid or impede organizational performance.

The conceptualization of a management audit as the measure and
evaluation of the total organizational performance is one thing; the
operationalization is another. Unfortunately, external management audits are not a uniform appraisal instrument. For, as Greenwood notes:

> Most audit checklists found in the business periodical litera-
> ture tend to be functional types, for specific departments, al-
> though a few comprehensive company-wide audits are also found.
> Some audits apply only to operating management and its functions
> and others apply to the board of directors.[32]

---

[29]Hodgetts, p. 214.

[30]Robert B. Buchele, "How To Evaluate A Firm," Californian Management
Review Fall 1962 , p. 5.

[31]Lawrence B. Sawyer, "Operational Auditing," in Handbook for Auditors,
ed. James A. Cashin (New York: McGraw-Hill, 1971), pp. 51-53.

[32]Greenwood, p. 47.

The most widely recognized attempt to operationalize the management audit concept was developed by the American Institute of Management.[33] Table 3:2 illustrates the ten categories of the Management Audit of business organizations, as proposed by the American Institute of Management. Specific perimeters for rating levels of excellence in each of these areas is included.

TABLE 3:2

MANAGEMENT AUDIT CATEGORIES[34]

Category	Optimum Rating	Minimum for Excellence
Economic Function	1,000	750
Corporate Structure.........	500	375
Health of Earnings..........	600	450
Service to Stockholders.....	700	525
Research and Development....	800	600
Directorate Effectiveness...	800	600
Fiscal Policies.............	1,000	750
Production Efficiency.......	1,100	825
Sales Vigor.................	1,300	975
Executive Quality...........	2,200	1,650
Total Points	10,000	7,500

To determine overall performance, an organization is examined and rated in each of these ten areas. The resulting expression is a comparative statement of the worth of a particular management, in each department of managerial effort, related both to a norm for excellent

---

[33] American Institute of Management, Appraising a Management, pamphlet, 1, No. 21 (1950).

[34] Martindell, p. 83. This format has been utilized to conduct management audits on numerous organizations varying from the Catholic Church to California Packing Corporation and to Iowa Power and Light Company.

management and to a hypothetical measure of management perfection.
The theory rests upon the assumption that weakness in any single division of a management reflects failures of the management as a whole.[35]
Martindell in noting some of the salient features of the ten categories, states that

> These categories are in no sense pure variables. The same
> activities are considered in several of them, usually from
> different points of view....The relative weighting of the
> ten categories of the Management Audit has been arrived at
> comparatively, on an experience basis....The actual numbers
> assigned to each category of appraisal are only guides to the
> relative values of different management functions. They are
> not statistical measures.[36]

In 1968, Burton noted that it seemed likely that in the coming decade there would be an increasing demand for information about organizational performance, especially in the form of a management audit.[37]
His assessment appears correct.

A noteworthy characteristic of this system, as practiced by the
American Institute of Management, is that the concept of categori-
zation allows for comparative studies to be made between industries as
well. It is here that the management audit either in a complete or in
a preliminary, shortened form, shows promise for the business historian.

---

[35]Ibid., p. 3.

[36]Ibid.

[37]Burton, pp. 41-46.

CHAPTER IV

AN APPRAISAL GUIDE IN CONDUCTING A PRELIMINARY
MANAGEMENT AUDIT

In the previous chapters it has been demonstrated that the level
of management in any given organization is critically important to the
overall well-being of that organization. It follows that if a business
historian is to write accurately about any given organization, he must
somehow make judgments about the quality of the management.

It has been further suggested that the management audit concept
might be of use for analyzing organizations which existed in the past.
However, the use of management audit techniques in this manner has
been very limited, in spite of its apparent usefulness. One of the
problems seems to be that the standards of a certain time period and
environmental setting do not necessarily transfer to another. The
chief limiting factor, however, is the availability of evidence.

Professor Charles J. Kennedy is the pioneer in the application of
the management audit concept to historically significant organizations.[1] In his extensive history of the Boston and Maine Railroads

---

[1]Kennedy and his students were recognized in that respect by Lloyd K.
Marquis, president of the American Institute of Management, in his
dinner address of February 21, 1969. The full address is in Papers of
the Sixteenth Business History Conference, ed. Charles J. Kennedy (Lincoln: College of Business Administration, University of Nebraska-
Lincoln, 1969), pp. 38-48. Already cited are Charles Kennedy's
Management Appraisal for Historians and the 14 essays (including
some reprints) in his forthcoming volume, Railroad History: Entrepreneurial and Managerial Approach and Other Essays. Also, see

and its predecessors,[2] Kennedy developed and applied his own Management
Appraisal Guide based on the basic format of the AIM. (See Table 4:1)
He developed a different questionnaire, however, to allow for the
nature of the organization--a railroad--and the fact that he was dealing with the past--mainline railroads before 1870. Similar alterations in questionnaire design, especially for particular industries or
even non-profit organizations potentially could allow the business
historian to have a useful tool for more in-depth explanatory power.
In fact, as Kennedy notes,"if and whenever that is accomplished, then,
perhaps, historians would be able to reappraise the entire first
century or two of modern industrialization in all countries as to the
precise significance of the role of entrepreneurship and managerial
ability in the development of the industry."[3]

Because Kennedy's Management Appraisal Guide is the basis for the

his New Approach to the History of the American Business System
(Lincoln: College of Business Administration, University of Nebraska-
Lincoln, 1979). The most useful papers by his students are Bruce W.
Beloit, "Appraisal of Management Competence as a Measure in Economics
in Economic and Business History Research" (unpublished Master's
Thesis, Department of Economics, University of Nebraska, 1967);
Allen L. Bures, "The Management Audit Approach in Writing Business
History," read at the Symposium on Accounting and Management Apprais-
al in Writing Railroad History, April 29, 1978, Denver, Colorado.(All
papers of this symposium are scheduled for publication by EBHA Press
in late 1980), and "The Management Audit Approach in Writing Economic
History," read at the North American Economic Studies Association,
December 28, 1978, Mexico City, Mexico.

[2]For Kennedy's research on the Boston & Maine and the management
appraisal, refer to citations in bibliography.

[3]Kennedy, "Entrepreneurial and Managerial Appraisal... ." p. 7.

TABLE 4:1

KENNEDY'S MANAGEMENT APPRAISAL GUIDE FOR AMERICAN RAILROADS

Category	Optimum rating	Superior definitely above average, 85% and above	Average: not dangerously weak in any category, 84 - 70%	Harmful: certain functions were not performed effectively or were ignored, below 70%
I Entrepreneurship (6%)	600	510	509 - 421	490
II Social Responsibility (6%)	600	510	509 - 421	490
III Organizational Structure (5%)	500	425	424 - 351	350
IV Executive Ability (20%)	2,000	1,700	1,699 -1,401	1,400
V Directorate Effectiveness (8%)	800	680	679 - 561	560
VI Fiscal Policy (10%)	1,000	850	849 - 701	700
VII Operating Efficiency (11%)	1,100	935	934 - 771	770
VIII Marketing Effectiveness (13%)	1,300	1,105	1,104 - 911	910
IX Analysis, Planning, and Development (8%)	800	680	679 - 561	560
X Health of Earnings (6%)	600	510	509 - 421	420
XI Service to Stockholders (7%)	700	595	594 - 491	490
Total Points	10,000	8,500	8,499 -7,001	7,000

These categories are in no sense pure variables. Each of these categories deals with several functions. Some functions appear more than once because different aspects and interrelations with other functions have to be considered from other points of view. A central postulate is that the evaluation process must be comparative and historical. In addition, the theory of the A.I.M. management audit, which Kennedy follows, rests upon the assumption that any serious weakness in any single category of the management audit, if not corrected, in time will lead to failure of the management as a whole.

Although revision in the categories might be made for other industries, the basic format would remain the same. The actual numbers assigned to each category of appraisal are only guides to the relative values of different management functions. They are not statistical.

preliminary management audit proposed in this paper, a more complete explanation of this guide and how it can be used is in order.

CATEGORIES AND FUNCTIONS

For an understanding of management appraisal, a distinction must be drawn between the categories of the management audit and the functions they are designed to appraise. Kennedy's Management Appraisal Guide for American Railroads represented in Table 4:1 utilizes eleven major categories.[4] Of these, ten categories represent particular activities of the organization. The eleventh category, executive ability (designated Category IV) deals with the quality of top managers, their management philosophy, and the "fit" of both the individual managers and their philosophy in the organization given its environment.

It should be noted here that the categories are imaginary pigeonholes for separating the management role into its component parts, the purpose of which is to sort out evidence and facilitate analysis. In reality, these categories and the lines that divide them are somewhat arbitrary. As was pointed out in Chapter 2, the functions of an organization's management cannot actually be separated, so they tend to overlap and interlock in a total system. Moreover, some categories represent activities which affect virtually every area of the organization. In any analysis of the component parts of an organization, this must be

---

[4]This section leans heavily upon the works of Charles J. Kennedy and the American Institute of Management. See especially American Institute of Management, The Management Audit Bookshelf, 12 vols. (New York: American Institute of Management, 1959); and Charles J. Kennedy's works cited in note 1 of this chapter.

taken into consideration.

With this in mind, the eleven categories used in Kennedy's Management Appraisal Guide--the same categories to be used to demonstrate the preliminary management audit technique--are defined here. In addition, certain selected questions designed to illuminate the various categories will be mentioned, using sentences from Kennedy's Guide without indicating them as quotations.[5]

I. ENTREPRENEURSHIP (6%)

To refer to any policy makers in an organization one could use the term "entrepreneur," and could call their business functions "entrepreneurship." Cochran's definition of entrepreneurship as the function performed by those responsible for the inauguration, maintenance, or direction of a profit-oriented enterprise will be utilized in the study.[6] This has required a redefinition of a largely archaic term.[7]

---

[5]This is done with Professor Kennedy's permission. See Appendix A, below, for Kennedy's complete questionnaire.

[6]Thomas C. Cochran, Railroad Leaders, 1845 - 1890: The Business Mind in Action (Cambridge, Mass: Harvard University Press, 1953), pp. 8-9.

[7]Cochran, p. 8, gives a brief history of the term "entrepreneur" and its varied meanings. In the French tradition, begun by Richard Cantillon in the eighteenth century, the entrepreneur was the person who brought together the resources needed for production, and combined them to secure products for sale. Classical English economic theory, however, was more preoccupied with aggregates and the operation of impersonal forces. It was not until the 1930s that the term was more frequently used, when "historians became interested in the nature of business leadership, /and/ needed a term that would cover the functions of both professional executives and the older type of owner-manager, that is, one that would coincide with real activities in business. Inspired by Arthur H. Cole, these historian decided to redefine the entrepreneur, to call his activities entrepreneurship, and his functions entrepreneurial."

Questions such as the following are used in this category: What did
the railroad attempt and accomplish in interline freight traffic?
What did the railroad perceive as an opportunity in carrying mail, parcels, and small lots of freight? Did the managers continually scruti-
nize (and revitalize) their plan to keep in touch with changing
realities?

II. SOCIAL RESPONSIBILITY (6%)

This category attempts to determine the public value of the organization. This value is not defined in dollars or balance sheet terms.
Rather, it comprises such intangibles as the organization's reputation
and management's view of the purpose of the enterprise. In this category, management is evaluated on the one hand for what its purposes
are, and on the other for how it carries them out.

The idea of social responsibility is that decision-makers are
obligated to take actions which protect and improve the welfare of
society as a whole along with their own interests.[8] Chris Argyris
states that all organizations have three essential core activities.
These are (1) achieving objectives, (2) maintaining the internal
system, and (3) adapting to the external environment.[9] The "economic
man" concept tends to emphasize the first two core activities; however,
being socially responsive emphasizes adapting to the external environment and thus taking an open systems perspective.[10]

---

[8]Keith Davis and Robert L. Blomstrom, Business and Society: Environment
and Responsibility (New York: McGraw-Hill, 1975), p. 6.

[9]Chris Argyris, Integrating the Individual and the Organization (New
York: John Wiley & Sons, Inc., 1964), p. 120.

[10]See Chapter II, Figure 3.

Some of the questions posed to appraise social responsibility
are: Where, how, and to what extent did this railroad contribute a
heretofore unmet need in passenger transportation, such as commuters,
local, and interline? Did the railroad cooperate with the communities,
such as providing grade crossings, attractive depots and grounds, and
desired schedules? What did the railroad do for its employees besides
merely employing them? What was the railroad's reputation as a business concern, especially in its relations to the local community? Did
the railroad or its management participate in projects sponsored by
other organizations in the community or by the town or city government? In the area served by the railroad, what were the changes in
population and agricultural and industrial production? How and to what
extent did the railroad contribute to the actual expansion of markets?

To summarize, the organization's choice of how to serve the
economy, its social role, and its moral and ethical standards are what
are analyzed in this category.

III. ORGANIZATIONAL STRUCTURE (5%)

This category evaluates management's ability to organize the cooperation necessary for carrying out the purposes of the enterprise.
In any continuing organization, an established method of accomplishing
goals ultimately results in a formal organizational structure. In a
railroad, this is determined by the way in which responsibility and
authority are assigned. In addition, it includes the establishment of
distinct lines of formal and informal informational flows.

The quality of organizational structure can be gauged from answers
to such questions as the following: What positions did the president

hold? (President of company, president of board, chairman of finance committee, etc.) Did the directors formulate any policy or merely approve what the president and one or two other men presented? Did the railroad engage outside services, such as legal services, financing, stock transfer, production of engines and rolling stock? Did one or a few stockholders dominate the management? What were the titles and jurisdiction of the chief officials? Was there a clear distinction between responsibility and authority? Was there any indication of concern about organizational change to improve the effectiveness of the company?

The organizational structure should be appropriate to the specific undertaking given environmental considerations. Each organization must develop its structure according to its own needs. The structure should change to remain viable as conditions dictate. This is the key to quality in organization.

IV. EXECUTIVE ABILITY (20%)

This category is the most important of the eleven divisions of the management audit because the quality of performance in the other ten depends upon the thinking and actions of the executive group. The other ten are examined separately so that the effective results of the efforts of the individuals in management may be appraised, but the analysis of these officials themselves is important to management appraisal.

Foresight and alertness in grouping the significance of changing conditions is one of the central requirements. Another is to achieve a balance between adaptivity and maintenance. Adaptability encour-

ages flexibility to the external and internal environments whereas
maintenance attempts to stop the organization from changing so rapidly
that it is thrown out of balance, so as to forestall entropy. Also
considered are the selection and training aspects of other levels of
management. What appeared to be the practice or plan for recruiting,
training, compensating, and promoting officials? Was the communication and teamwork between the officials themselves and between the
officials and other employees of high or low quality? Was there a
reasonable delegation of authority? Did the authority delegated
match responsibility in every respect? Was there nepotism in the organization? Did the full-time officials engage in any public activities? Was there any evidence of provision for executive succession?
How able was the president (or whoever was the top full-time
executive)?

V. DIRECTORATE EFFECTIVENESS (8%)

In this category is evaluated the organization's board of
directors. Was it actually--not just formally--performing the trustee
function for both owners and public with which it was charged? The
board assumes ultimate legal and moral responsibility for the conduct
of the organization. This calls for the board to act as a central
authority for the guidance of management and for the direction of the
organization toward predetermined goals.

Such questions as the following help to determine directorate
effectiveness: Who were the members of the board and how long was
each one a director? Any evidence as to why each one was on the
board? Did they represent a wide range of background and points of

view? Did the directors direct, or did they merely pass upon proposals formulated by full-time officials? Did the directors, through committees, engage in activities that could have been delegated to full-time officials? To what extent did the president or any other one or two members dominate the board? Any evidence if the directors truly acted as concerned and responsible trustees for the stockholders? Did the directors appear to actually select the chief officials or did they merely give their assent to recommendations by the president or other dominant members?

VI. FISCAL POLICY (10%)

The objective of sound fiscal policy is to conserve, employ, and account for the resources of the organization so that funds are available when needed to achieve the organization's short and long range goals. This requires sound accounting, adequate control of resources, forecasting and budgeting of income and expenditures, suitable scheduling of capital outlays and returns, timely and accurate reporting of conditions, and maintenance of appropriate statistical and financial analysis to enable the organization to have available necessary information.

Such questions as the following will help to determine the quality of fiscal management: What was the ratio of debt to paid-in capital stock? Was the debt largely funded or unfunded? What was the provision or practice to finance the replacement of rolling stock, track, and buildings? How was expansion financed and what changes occurred in the capital structure? How much attention was given to the equivalent of the modern concepts of (1) operating ratio, (2) times fixed

charges earned, and (3) the percentage available for dividends? Was
fiscal policy the reason that the dividend rate and the market price of
the stock were not higher? Was there any form of budgetary control or
projecting of income and outgo? What were the trends in revenue per
ton-mile and revenue per passenger-mile? What was the policy on
insurance or lack of insurance?

The strength which a management can develop through the proper
exercise of fiscal policy gives it an advantage in times of stress or
business decline. In essence this category includes the organization's
financial structure, its organization for developing fiscal policies
and controls, and the application of these policies and controls. Consequently, the major area of interest is the providing, controlling,
and husbanding of capital.

VII. OPERATING EFFICIENCY (11%)

The AIM termed this category production efficiency. Evaluating
production efficiency has obvious importance in appraising a manu-
facturing concern; however, its counterpart--operating efficiency--
is equally important to transportation concerns. The quality of
management in this category is evidenced by its ability to utilize
equipment effectively. These results depend upon choices a management
has made in the technological and manpower areas. To appraise the
evidence that management has met these challenges, questions such as
the following are utilized: How much attention was given to the modern
concepts of (1) the transportation ratio, (2) average freight trainload, (3) freight traffic density, (4) passenger traffic density? Did
the management appear to be interested in the concept of productivity?

Did the superintendent (or general manager if there was one) operate mainly in the yards or from behind an office desk? Was there a significant difference in local load-factors by route segments, outbound and inbound? How were employee grievances handled? Any indications of labor disputes? What indication was there of anything resembling modern job evaluation and merit rating? What is the evidence of labor turnover?

In summary, this category emphasizes the need for management to be alert to income efficiency and to meet the challenge of competition in the use of "machinery and material management" as well as "manpower management."

VIII. MARKETING EFFECTIVENESS (13%)

This category encompasses the entire marketing function: market analysis, planning, product, promotion, place, price and the manpower factors related to these activities. No other single function is as closely interrelated with the organization's activities than is marketing. Earnings, dividends, efficiency, finance, and over-all organizational strategy--including its ethical and moral guidelines-- are bound up with its marketing effort. Marketing effectiveness, under which are evaluated the avenues by which goods and services are translated into profit is the determining factor in the appraisal of an organization's activity.

Such questions as the following aid in appraising marketing effectiveness: How did the management determine the freight rates and the passenger rates, both local and interline? What did the company do in the way of promotion? Was there any evidence of what has since been called market research and analysis? Was there any constructive policy to improve shipper and passenger relations? Did the management appear to be aggressive in sales vigor or was there an attitude of merely serving the customer when he arrived or said he had a shipment?

In summary, an appraisal of marketing effectiveness leans heavily on the evidence that the organization handles its marketing function aggressively, ethically, and effectively based upon the marketing concept of meeting customer needs at a reasonable profit.

IX. ANALYSIS, PLANNING, AND DEVELOPMENT (8%)

Management's provision for the origination of ideas, processes, services, and procedures is appraised in this category. Analysis, planning, and development should include not only research and development connected with technology but also the investigation of such areas as organization, communications, systems, and executive development. The attitude of top management is significant.

Appraisal in this category should consider questions such as the following: Was the railroad responsible for any pioneering developments in passenger service and rates? Was the railroad responsible for any pioneering developments in the movement of freight? What did the railroad do to improve the design, effectiveness, or lower cost of roadbeds, superstructure, and bridges? Does the management or do certain officials cooperate with any professional organizations or with informal groups of railroad officials in what has since been called research and development? What evidence is there of trade books and periodicals read by the management, including the chief mechanic?

X. HEALTH OF EARNINGS (6%)

What determines management's quality in this category is its ability to sustain company earnings and growth over time, even during fluctuations in the business cycle and in the face of competition. In addition, the organization's profits should be compared against those of other similar organizations in the same industry as well as against its own true potential. Analysis of balance sheets and income statements of previous years affords evidence of management's performance. Consequently, answers to questions such as the following aid in appraising management in the health of earnings category: After recasting the income statement, what percent of the railway operating revenue was available for dividends? Using the same recasted income statement, how much has been carried to the surplus or other unencumbered funds after the payment of dividends? Do the earnings show only a relation to the growth of the population and national income or does a part of the earnings come from aspects of business new to this road? During the most recent years of depressed business conditions what was the company's record or earnings? How did that compare with other railroads? Approximately what percent of the railroad's business came from low paying types of business? Did the earnings show an increasing rate of return on equity or at least the previous rate of return on each new addition of capital?

If management has met the test of health of earnings, the evidence is strong that the organization's economic function is a valid one.

XI. SERVICE TO STOCKHOLDERS (7%)

Appraisal of performance in this category consists of genuine recognition by management of the fact that the stockholders own the business. Performance in this category will determine the organization's access to equity capital when it is needed. The directors and managers have an implied mandate, for example, to safeguard their invested principal from unnecessary risks or impairment, enhance the principal, distribute profits as dividends at reasonable and safe levels, and keep stockholders adequately informed.

The quality of management in this category can be gleaned from answers to questions like the following: What percentage of earnings available for dividends was paid out as dividends annually the past several decades? Did the railroad ever withhold expenditures for (1) maintenance, (2) renewal, or (3) depreciation funds in order to pay dividends? Did the railroad borrow to pay dividends? What was the practice of the management to enhance both earnings and net worth? What did the management do to maintain the company's securities at price levels reflecting the needs of owners to sell or buy? Were the annual reports to the stockholders sufficiently informative and accurate so that the owners of the securities could make rational decisions and participate properly in the stockholders' meetings? Were the dividends so high that in the future the railroad would be unable to "replace" its worn-out rolling stock (including locomotives) and railway?

THE SCALE OF EVALUATION AND WEIGHTING

The above summaries of each of the eleven categories deal with several functions. There is no category in which excellence or its opposite does not impact upon most if not all other categories. For example, fiscal policy is a category in which the functions examined impact upon planning, budgeting, research, marketing, personnel relations, etc. Another such category is marketing effectiveness. In fact, what management does in its marketing aspect is perhaps more interrelated and interdependent with other functions than any other single category. The category of executive ability, is, of course, the most striking of all in the pervasive influence the performances evaluated in it have over the whole organization being studied. The analyst must view the organization as a whole by utilizing a systems approach and yet study each category separately.

THE PRELIMINARY MANAGEMENT AUDIT PROCEDURE

The preliminary management audit paradigm has been posited as a workable, adequate, acceptable procedure to gather and analyze data to allow longitudinal comparisons between managements of various firms in a particular industry. The use of such a methodological tool as an aid in the writing of business history rests upon the propositions that (1) managements vary between business units (railroads), (2) environmental circumstances account at least partially but not wholly for variations in the performance of each firm (railroad), (3) different managements may be more or less effective in differing environments, and (4) such differences in managements help explain varying roles played by different business firms (railroads).

Essential to both Kennedy's management appraisal and a preliminary management audit is the determination of what constitutes the various levels of management excellence or lack thereof given environmental

circumstances. Such determinations are based upon the findings in
total as well as from each of the eleven categories individually. It
is clear that the categories are not of equal importance nor are they
in any sense pure variables. Nevertheless, the theory behind the
management audit rests upon the assumption that weakness in any single
division of management reflects shortcomings of the management as a
whole. Although the point system of evaluation has been developed
as guides to the relative values of different management functions,
the values derived should not be regarded as measures subject to
statistical computation.

At this point something should be said about the primary differences between Kennedy's management appraisal technique and the preliminary management audit posed and demonstrated in this paper. As was
mentioned earlier, the technique of Kennedy's Management Appraisal
Guide is central to both; it is the way this guide is used that
differs.

In conducting a complete management appraisal, a historian would
apply this guide to a firm or organization using every source of
information he could possibly find. This would include all primary
and secondary sources available, including, probably, many old manuscripts and miscellaneous records which survived from the period. The
preliminary management audit uses mostly secondary sources and annual
reports.

Another way in which these two methods differ is in the amount of
data generated before conclusions are drawn. For a complete management appraisal, the guide is applied to the firm or organization for

every single year of the life of the organization covered in the study.[11] The preliminary management audit, on the other hand, is more of a "sampler," gathering data at periodic intervals. The preliminary management audit demonstrated in this paper is based on an analysis of a forty year period, with data gathered for every tenth year.

Compared to Kennedy's entrepreneurial and management appraisal technique, the preliminary management audit might appear to be a "short cut," a less refined technique which would accomplish the same ends. However, the preliminary management audit is just as the term suggests: it is "preliminary" and therefore not adequate for writing a complete history of any specific firm or organization. For this, a complete management appraisal would be necessary. Rather, the preliminary management audit is a tool which can aid in initial analysis of a particular organization or group of organizations in a specific time period. It is meant to give the scholar adequate explanatory power and findings without the time-consuming task of a total management appraisal of each business unit.

The preliminary management audit procedure used in this paper is composed of two distinct yet related phases:

1. Generating a data base
2. The analysis phase

Generating a data base. Three main sources of information are utilized in the preliminary management audit of early American railroads demonstrated in this paper, namely Poor's Manual of the Rail-

---

[11]Kennedy's study goes from 1830-1955. If financial support is obtained, it will be continued to the present.

roads of the United States,[12] Annual Reports of the Board of Directors
to their Stockholders,[13] and quality secondary works on individual
railroads.[14]

A questionnaire (see Appendix A) consisting of 5-20 questions for
each of the eleven categories of the Guide (Table I), is applied to
five mainline railroads as completely and as accurately as possible
based upon the above resources. Given the years under consideration
(1870, 1880, 1890 and 1900), this type of procedure is the only one
available, as personal interviews and responses to questionnaires from

---

[12]Henry V. Poor, Poor's Manual of the Railroads of the United States
(New York, 1870-1 to 1902). The University of Nebraska-Lincoln
Library's Charles J. Kennedy Railroad Collection, has a complete set
for 1868-1924.

[13]Annual Reports of the Board of Directors of the Chicago, Burlington &
Quincy Railroad Company to the Stockholders, selected years 1870-1901;
Annual Reports of the Board of Directors of the Illinois Central Rail-
road to the Stockholders, selected years 1870-1901; Annual Reports of
the President and Directors of the Louisville & Nashville Railroad
Company to the Stockholders, selected years 1870-1901; Annual Reports
of the Board of Directors of the Atchison, Topeka and Santa Fe Rail-
road Company to the Stockholders, selected years 1870-1901; Annual
Reports of the Board of Directors of the Boston and Maine Railroad
Company to the Stockholders, selected years 1870-1901. The Charles
J. Kennedy Railroad collection of annual reports is incomplete; however, immediate attention is being given to the completion of the file.

[14]For example see: Maury Klein, History of the Louisville and Nashville
Railroad (New York: The Macmillan Company, 1972); Richard C. Overton,
Burlington Route (New York: Alfred A. Knopf, 1965); John F. Stover,
History of the Illinois Central (New York: The Macmillan Company,
1975); Keith Bryant, History of the Atchison, Topeka, and Santa Fe
(New York: Macmillan, 1960); Charles J. Kennedy, Chapters on the
Boston and Maine Railroad System, Volume I, Volume II, part I (Lin-
coln: University of Nebraska, 1978, 1979). This last book by Kennedy
is a preliminary draft of his forthcoming multi-volume study of the
Boston and Maine System. Volumes I and II were issued only to his
students and the members of the symposia referred to in note 1 of
this chapter and now both volumes are out of print.

corporation officials, methods used in present day management audits, obviously are impossible to obtain.[15]

The Analysis Phase. Once the data is gathered, and information has been generated about each of the five railroads in all eleven categories, the management of each of five railroads will be rated as superior, average or harmful for each tenth year of the forty year period under study.

The completed questionnaires are also useful for analyzing component as well as overall organizational management. Two main sets of criteria determine judgments: the needs of the organization and the comparative performance of other organizations and their managements. The comparative as well as individual organizational analysis has the potential to become " . . . a powerful diagnostic tool; and to serve the same purpose that a thorough physical check-up in a medical clinic does for an individual."[16] This comparative approach was utilized by

---

[15]The gathering of information by the AIM in their Management Audit is obtained in three ways: by questionnaire to be answered by the organization's officials, by review of the organization's annual reports and other publications, and by interviews conducted by one or more of the AIM's analysts with selected officials. These three means are blended in varying proportions. The usual general questionnaire is comprised of 301 questions. However, by use of special questionnaires adapted to specific industries and types or organizations, management audits have been conducted for educational and religious organizations, hospitals, and even entire geographic areas. Jackson Martindell's The Appraisal of Management (New York: Harper & Row, 1965) is recommended reading as well as Lloyd Marquis' article, "A Comprehensive Framework for Analyzing the Management of a Business Enterprise," in Papers of the Sixteenth Business History Conference.

[16]AIM, Manual of Excellent Managements, 10th ed. (New York: AIM, 1966), p. xiv.

Kennedy in his analysis and development of a comparative management appraisal of fifteen major railroads, 1840 - 1870.

Although some might claim that the conclusions drawn from this type of data are still subjective, and not subject to exact statistical measurement, this type of analysis is nonetheless more objective than conclusions based on mere intuition and speculation.

Chapter V, then, will illustrate the application and conclusions of the preliminary management audit as applied to the Atchison, Topeka, and Santa Fe; Boston and Maine; Chicago, Burlington and Quincy; Illinois Central; and the Louisville and Nashville for the years 1870, 1880, 1890 and 1900.

CHAPTER V

FINDINGS FROM A PRELIMINARY MANAGEMENT

AUDIT OF FIVE SELECTED RAILROADS

This chapter presents the findings from the application of the
preliminary management audit technique to five railroads: (1) the
Chicago, Burlington and Quincy, (2) the Illinois Central, (3) the
Atchison, Topeka and Santa Fe, (4) the Boston and Maine, and (5) the
Louisville and Nashville for the years of 1870, 1880, 1890 and 1900.
Only a few references will be made to the Boston and Maine in this
chapter because Chapter VI discusses that road in more detail.

Reference is made to selected accounting and related statistical
data for each railroad. See Appendix C. This data was developed
following Kennedy's method of compilation. See Appendix B. Such
data, although not all one might desire, does provide a basis for
textual analysis and a source of more detail. As Kennedy notes:

> Railroad managers and large investors during the first decades
> following the beginning of the first railroads frequently dis-
> cussed financial strength and operating efficiency but found
> them difficult to measure. Today's historian likewise is
> necessarily handicapped because of inadequate records and the
> impossibility of personal interviews. Although the extremes
> are easily discernible, the comparison of many early roads
> is most difficult yet necessary in order to understand the
> record of any one company and the development of the railroad
> industry.[1]

---

[1]For the uses of accounting and statistical data see especially:
Charles J. Kennedy, "Adjusting and Using Accounting Data as an Aid in
Writing Railroad History, Especially 1830-1860," presented to the

It should be emphasized that the findings portrayed in this chapter are very "preliminary" and in nowise on the same level of thoroughness as a complete management appraisal based on primary sources would be. Although a judgment of superior, average, or harmful is rendered for each railroad in each of the eleven categories for the years examined, such judgments were based on varying amounts of data. For example, there was a great deal of data available on most of the roads during the years examined regarding Category IV, executive ability. On the other hand, very little could be found in the area of Category III, organizational structure, for the Illinois Central, while data in this category was plentiful on the Chicago, Burlington and Quincy. Further, in some categories it was necessary to estimate from data of a preceding or subsequent year. As Kennedy notes, "obviously some points cannot be measured very adequately, but the limitations...apply to all the railroads...and do not seriously effect the rank of any one road in comparison with other roads."[2]

The secondary sources also varied in terms of the amount of data they disclosed. For example, the sources for the Boston and Maine, although highly interesting and illuminating, did not lend themselves

---

Lexington Group of Transportation Historians, Feb. 24, 1977, Columbus, Ohio, and published in Charles J. Kennedy, Excerpts from Kennedy's Boston and Maine (Lincoln: University of Nebraska, 1978), pp. 77-86. See p. 85. This paper will be reprinted in Kennedy's forthcoming Railroad History: Entrepreneurial and Managerial Appraisal and Other Essays.

[2] Charles J. Kennedy, Chapters on the Boston & Maine Railroad System, Volume 2, Part 1 (Lincoln, Nebraska: College of Business Administration, University of Nebraska-Lincoln, 1979), p. 363.

particularly well to this kind of inquiry.[3] On the other hand,
Overton's Chicago, Burlington and Quincy was quite helpful. These
limitations will be recognized in the next chapter.

Each of the categories, then, is evaluated by applying appropriate
questions to the data available. A summary of the overall findings
is given in Figure 5:9 at the end of this chapter. Following the
assessment of the roads, some general illustrations are given for each
category to demonstrate the kind of data on which the judgments were
based. These examples are purely illustrative; they are not meant to
be either exclusive or inclusive. Some roads are mentioned in some of
the various categories; others are not. The illustrations are added
simply to give the reader some idea of the kind of data available.

I. ENTREPRENEURSHIP

	1870	1880	1890	1900
A T & S F	Superior	Average	Harmful	Average
B & M	Superior	Superior	Average	Average
C B & Q	Superior	Superior	Average	Average
I C	Average	Average	Average	Average
L & N	Superior	Average	Average	Average

---

[3]Kennedy's work in his Chapters . . . , Vol. 2 (a preliminary draft of
his final study of the Boston & Maine System), and in his unpublished
statistics, is to be contrasted with the data gleaned from the following sources: Francis C. B. Bradlee, The Boston and Maine Railroad:
A History of the Maine Road, With Its Tributory Lines (Salem, Mass.:
Essex Institute, 1921); Edward C. Kirkland, Men, Cities and Transportation: A Study in New England History, Volumes I and II (Cambridge,
Mass.: Harvard University Press, 1948); Alvin F. Harlow, Steelways
of New England (New York: Creative Age Press, Inc., 1946); and
George P. Baker, The Formation of the New England Railroad System
(Cambridge, Mass.: Harvard University Press, 1949).

Entrepreneurship has been defined as the functions performed by
persons responsible for the inauguration, maintenance, or direction of
a profit-oriented business.[4] Not only does management need to manage
and improve what is already known but it needs to redirect resources
from areas of low or diminishing results to areas of high or increasing
results. In reflecting upon the role of the entrepreneur, Drucker
notes that the entrepreneur has to slough off yesterday and to render
obsolete what already exists and is already known. He has to create
tomorrow.[5] How successful were the managements of these railroads in
creating the "business of tomorrow"?

Perhaps one of the best illustrations, which in some ways is
representative of all five roads in their infancy, is provided by
Colonel Cyrus K. Holliday, the early entrepreneur of the Atchison,
Topeka, and Santa Fe. The completion of seven miles of roads in 1869
marked the occasion of a speech by Holliday in which he began to pre-
dict the future of the western railroads. "Fellow citizens," he pro-
claimed, "the coming tide of immigration will flow along these lines
and, like an ocean wave, advance upon the sides of the Rockies and
dash their foamy crests down upon the Pacific. See, there rolls the
broad Pacific and on its breast are the ships of the Santa Fe riding

---

[4]Thomas C. Cochran, Railroad Leaders 1845-1890: The Business Mind in
Action (Cambridge, Mass: Harvard University Press, 1953), pp. 8-9.

[5]Peter F. Drucker, Management: Tasks, Responsibilities, Practices
(New York: Harper and Row, 1974), p. 45.

in from the Orient."[6] Such was Colonel Holliday's vision of the
Atchison, Topeka, and Santa Fe becoming a giant railway network, a
transcontinental railroad, creating the business of tomorrow."

If Holliday's enthusiasm seems unbounded and unrealistic to the
reader, it should be remembered that an optimistic belief in progress
was a dominant thread in American life in the forty years before and
the thirty years after the Civil War.[7] Nationalism and expansionism
combined with a sense of adventure and a desire for trade and markets
made visions such as Colonel Holliday's commonplace.

In 1900, thirty-two years after ground was broken in Topeka the
Atchison, Topeka, and Santa Fe had grown to a system of 7,425 miles.[8]
In retrospect, several factors were noteworthy during this expansion.[9]
First, those individuals who headed the company were railroad men who
wanted to build and run a railroad. Second, much of the line was built
in advance of traffic. Lines were built where trade had the best prospects of developing. Third, construction was above average in quality.
Fourth, competition among railroads occasioned construction of some
lines long before traffic warranted. Areas had to be tapped; those
companies which hesitated lost traffic. Fifth, as population in-

---

[6]Keith L. Bryant, Jr., History of the Atchison, Topeka & Santa Fe
Railway (New York: Macmillan, 1974), p. 2.

[7]Ibid.

[8]See Appendix E:1.

[9]This analysis leans heavily upon L. L. Waters, Steel Trails to Santa
Fe (Lawrence, Kansas: University of Kansas Press, 1950).

creased a necessity developed for branch lines and feeders to fill the gaps between the main lines. Thus, the Atchison, Topeka, and Santa Fe built numerous feeders. Sixth, rapid expansion in undeveloped areas was fraught with the danger of adding lines which would prove undesirable. A few of these additions turned out to be imprudent and will be considered later. Seventh, a railroad system was developed which spread from Chicago over the southwest quarter of the nation. The system served two states, Texas and California, which were to develop largely in the years to come and provide long hauls over natural routes of commerce to and from Chicago. There was nothing that Holliday envisioned which did not come true. To the contrary, the Atchison, Topeka and Santa Fe management demonstrated those entrepreneurial talents necessary in creating the business of tomorrow--the inaugurating, maintaining and directing a profit-oriented business.

Similar entrepreneural talents were demonstrated by early managements of the Chicago, Burlington and Quincy. When James F. Joy became president of the Chicago, Burlington and Quincy, he had, among other things, two specific assets which were to stand him in good stead during his tenure.[10] One was the confidence of his fellow directors; the other was his abundant energy. As early as 1858 John Maury Forbes assured Joy that he "had a foundation in my esteem and respect that I am sure nothing can shake."[11] The practical result of this opinion

[10]Richard C. Overton, Burlington Route: A History of the Burlington Lines (New York: Alfred A. Knopf, 1965), p. 86.

[11]Forbes to Joy, March 1858, quoted in M. C. McConkey: "Manuscript Biography of James F. Joy," in Overton, p. 86.

was that Joy was to have virtually a free hand in the management of
the property.

Under Joy's tutelage, the Chicago, Burlington and Quincy exempli-
fied that, despite the giddy competitive atmosphere and the constant
temptation to expand, the company should be prepared to respect the
feelings of other neighboring roads and limit its own expansion to
territory that already was or logically could be earmarked as its own.
This policy was predicated upon the assumption that a rapidly growing
country would supply enough business for everyone, and that it was
much wiser to handle such business in the most efficient and profitable
way possible than to dissipate energies in unnecessary competitive warfare.[12] Here was Joy's philosophy in a nutshell; nor did his theme
change as time continued. "In a country like the west," he told the
stockholders in 1869, "it is impossible to remain stationary. If the
companies owning and managing roads there do not meet the wants of the
adjoining country and aid in its development, other alliances are sure
to be found which end in rival roads, and damage to existing interests."[13]

This philosophy appears to have been shared by managements of the
Chicago, Burlington and Quincy and was the long-run view of business
that Forbes had always championed. Overton notes that Forbes would
not build a "speculator's railroad," but instead built solid properties and took a deep interest in land grants. He, as well as Brooks

[12]Overton, p. 154.

[13]Annual Report of the Board of Directors of the Chicago, Burlington
& Quincy Railroad Company (Chicago, 1869), p. 20.

and Von Nortwick, "were concerned with building up a community with which they and their railroads expected to be permanently identified."[14]

Although H. V. Newcomb was president of the Louisville and Nashville less than a year, he, too, exhibited entrepreneurial elements of "creating the business of tomorrow" but in a fashion somewhat dissimilar from managements of the Atchison, Topeka and Santa Fe and the Chicago, Burlington and Quincy. In constructing his system, Newcomb gained a stranglehold on Nashville and other interior points, strengthened the perimeters of the territory, and penetrated some new markets regarded by him as logically belonging to the Louisville and Nashville. To be sure, his policies had aroused antagonism among some rival roads, state legislatures, and shippers and promoted the development of the term "Newcomb's Octopus."[15] By 1880 Newcomb announced that the Louisville and Nashville system "is now complete and no consolidation or amalgamation with any company is contemplated, nor are any acquisitions contemplated."[16] He was not exactly correct.

Newcomb subscribed to the territorial strategy thesis--to define the railroad's territory and render it impregnable. He insisted that virtually every recent acquisition was not only a benefit but a necessity to the territory. In clear, unmistakable language he maintained that the Louisville and Nashville had become "invulnerable to the

[14]Overton, p. 154.

[15]Maury Klein, History of the Louisville and Nashville Railroad (New York : Macmillan 1972), p. 159.

[16]Commercial and Financial Chronicle (March 13, 1880), p. 273, as quoted by Klein, p. 160.

attacks and assaults of any of its competition" and that "the construction of new and competitive lines /¯would be_/ incapable of in-
flicting serious damage or loss of business."[17] Contrary to his claims,
however, Newcomb did not seal off the territory; he actually multiplied
the possible areas of dispute and merely enlarged the battlefield.[18]

The men who succeeded Newcomb after 1880 represented a new breed
of entrepreneurs. Most of them were financiers with little practical
railroad experience, and their accession marked a beginning of the
trend to separate the functions of financial and operational control.[19]
One of the most significant aspects of this charge was in the growth of
interterritorial competition. It constituted the logical alternative
to the territorial concept. The new strategy appeared to promise
flexibility. It would take time for new local traffic to develop
sufficiently to turn a profit, and only a system large enough to cover
losses in one territory with gains in another seemed able to buy that
time. Such was the situation when Milton H. Smith began his thirty-
seven year presidency of the Louisville and Nashville in 1884.

Smith was an entrepreneur in the full sense of Cochran's definition, being responsible for the inauguration, maintenance, and direction of the Louisville and Nashville through 1921. His ideas for
creating the business of tomorrow lay in his developmental strategy of
low rates and a modest profit margin. "While higher rates would have

---

[17]Annual Report of the President and Directors of the Louisville and
Nashville Railroad Company (Louisville, 1880), pp. 7-8.

[18]Klein, p. 170.

[19]Ibid., p. 172.

given a better return on capital invested," Smith explained in 1869, "they would probably have prevented development, or else produced active competition by other roads which would have been built in that section."[20] Smith's managerial talents will be further illustrated in Category IV, managerial effectiveness.

II. SOCIAL RESPONSIBILITY

	1870	1880	1890	1900
A T & S F	Average	Average	Harmful	Superior
B & M	Average	Average	Average	Average
C B & Q	Average	Average	Superior	Superior
I C	Average	Average	Average	Average
L & N	Average	Average	Harmful	Average

To know what a business is we have to start with its purpose. As Drucker notes, "the purpose of business must lie in society since business enterprise is an organ of society."[21] In essence, management is evaluated not only for what its purposes are but also how it carries them out. Stated differently, one concern deals with what the firm or organization in question does for society, the other with what the firm can do to society.

The firm and its management, existing to provide a service to

---

[20]Annual Report of the President and Directors of the Louisville & Nashville Railroad Company (Louisville, 1889),p. 13.

[21]Drucker, Management, p. 61.

society, necessarily needs to be part of society. It must be located
in a community and be a neighbor, usually it is a competitor, and it
must operate within a total environmental setting--social, political,
economic and technological. It has to employ resources to do its work
and its social impact inevitably goes far beyond the specific contribution it exists to make.

By 1870 the public was becoming "highly critical of railroad
management."[22] The depression of the seventies and the Grange movement hostilities waned somewhat in the early eighties but as Cochran
notes "it remained a force to be reckoned with by managers in every
section."[23] In an 1883 memorandum from James Clark (Illinois Central
president) to Fish (soon-to-be president), the view of an adverse
public attitude as inherent in the railroad situation is stated: "The
people are in favor of building a new road and do what they can to
promote it. After it is once built and fixed then the policy of the
people is usually in opposition."[24] Why? Although perhaps not entirely inclusive, three main points might be posited: (1) The person-
alities of some railroad entrepreneurs, (2) a suspicion of corporations
in general, and (3) monopolistically competitive or oligopolistic
competition in particular.

One must be careful not to judge managements of an earlier time
period by today's standards. What was "right" then may be condemned

---

[22]Cochran, p. 184.

[23]Ibid.

[24]Clarke, president, to Fish, vice-president, September 13, 1883,
as quoted in Cochran, p. 184.

today. For example, since the early 1960s the meaning of the words
"social responsibility of business" has changed radically.[25] Earlier
discussions of social responsibility centered in three areas: (1)
the relationship between private ethics and public ethics, (2) the responsibility which the employer bears toward his employees by virtue of
his wealth and power and (3) the role of management with respect to
"culture," community development, and philanthropy.[26]

An illucidating example of the Chicago, Burlington and Quincy's
President Perkins' concept of social responsibility centers around the
almost unbelievable action by which he saved the First National Bank of
Lincoln from collapse.[27] Late in 1895 it was discovered that unless
confidence could be restored to the institution, the First National
would have to close its doors. At that time Perkins was a small stockholder with a total investment of approximately $15,000. Had the bank
closed, the economy of the South Platte Valley would have been adverse-
ly affected. Unbeknown to Perkins, the stockholders, in a desperate
move to win public confidence, elected him a director and gave the fact
wide publicity. The end result was that no runs were made on the bank
funds and the First National survived the crisis.

Perkins could have repudiated this unauthorized action, but those
close to the scene pointed out the perilous condition of the bank and
he consented to let his name remain. In fact, before he was through,

---

[25]Drucker, Management, p. 313.

[26]Ibid., pp. 313-325.

[27]This section draws heavily from the analysis provided by Overton,
pp. 242-243.

he not only paid the stockhold assessments but raised over a million and a third dollars by selling his personal securities at a financial sacrifice. Not until 1899 was the First National on a firm basis but leaving Perkins with questionable assets, which by the time of his death in 1907 offset less than half the funds he had earlier supplied.

The point of the illustration is impressive. Perkins' personal liability as a stockholder was approximately $15,000. He could have refused to serve as a director. But because the region and the railroad would have suffered if the First National failed, he sacrificed a sizeable portion of his personal savings. In fact, he not only refused to let others share the burden but flatly forbade anyone to make public what he had done. The action taken was not an official one but it reveals as little else could Perkins' character and his sense of obligation both to the Chicago, Burlington and Quincy and the community and its service area.

Since public opinion and good will were desirable in the communities served by the roads, illustrations related to such are in order. Perkins emphasized that "it is quite unwise for railroads to quarrel with communities if it can be avoided."[28] Undoubtedly public opinion was also used as an excuse to stop or avoid doing things that management opposed for other reasons. The Illinois Central's Fish, for example, used public reaction to the Morgan rate conferences of 1889 and 1890 as an excuse for his road's noncooperation.[29]

---

[28]Perkins, president, to Potter, vice-president, June 11, 1885, as quoted in Cochran, p. 158.

[29]Fish, president, to Jeffery, general manager, January 22, 1889, as quoted in Cochran, p. 158.

Media for creating good will were many under Ripley president of
the Atchison, Topeka and Santa Fe. His management team believed,
within limits, that good pay and working conditions were economical.
Benefits were extended to the employees as rapidly as company resources
permitted with the end result being the development of a broad program
of social security. This lead Waters to note that the "company developed a spirit of loyalty and cooperation that was never equaled before
or after."[30] Other examples of employee assistance on the Atchison,
Topeka and Santa Fe included the railroad Y.M.C.A., hospital association, and employees' magazine, an apprentice system, improved dis-
ciplinary methods, a pension program, reading rooms, a death benefit
plan, and, lastly, countless other schemes for acquainting workers with
their supervisors and administrators.[31]

Ripley's outspokenness and blunt manner often brought him and the
railroad unfavorable publicity. For example, at an Interstate Commerce
Committee hearing in Chicago, Ripley was asked what reasonable rates
were. He answered,

> There never was any better definition than that which was given
> many years ago by somebody and which has been used as a by-word
> and a reproach ever since, namely, "What the traffic will bear."
> That does not mean all the traffic will bear, it does not mean
> all that can be extorted or squeezed out of it, but what the
> traffic will bear having regard to the freest possible movement
> of commodities, the least possible burden on the producer and the
> consumer, the middleman can take care of himself.[32]

---

[30]Waters, p. 292.

[31]Ibid., pp. 292-337.

[32]Albro Martin, Enterprise Denied: Origins of the Decline of the American Railroads, 1897-1917 (New York: Columbia University Press, 1971),
pp. 200-201.

His answer proved costly --"charge what the traffic will bear!"
Taken out of context and ignoring the explanation which followed,
Ripley and his road would pay a heavy price for such an "unsocially
responsible" statement. While one member of the Illinois Central
called Ripley's testimony "most statesmanlike," the "progressives" had
all the evidence they needed to prove "greed and avarice" on the part
of railway management.[33]

The role played by Fred Harvey in the area of social responsibility can be mentioned here, although he was not in the strict sense of
the word a member of the Atchison, Topeka and Santa Fe management.[34]
Harvey's role as purveyor of fine foods has been described as the
"greatest civilizing influence in the west."[35] Quite as unusual as
this influence on social development was the association between the
Harvey and Santa Fe companies. The two complemented each other and
worked in a manner almost "unparalled in the history of American business." The two were never legal partners yet "companies have never
cooperated or labored any more closely in each other's behalf."[36]
William Strong and Edward Ripley found in Harvey a significant asset
and not only did the railroad and Harvey cooperate and profit, but the
public they served also benefited.

By the late 1800s the ability to interact successfully with the

---

[33]Bryant, p. 209.

[34]The role Fred Harvey played will be expanded in Category VIII -
marketing effectiveness.

[35]Waters, p. 261.

[36]Ibid.

roads' various public obviously had become an important part of the executive role. Railroads individually or collectively had major impacts upon the socio-economic life of most communities. Consequently, the roads' officialdom could not avoid public scrutiny of their social responsibilities. In an imperfectly competitive industry character-ized by rapid growth and large scale firms never before experienced by management or the public, it is little wonder that difficulties arose. There was little time to develop a uniform philosophy of their proper relations to their public.

The railroad managements seem first and foremost to be prag-matists.[37] The question was what would work well to the advantage of management or the company? A theory to justify the choice could be developed later. The strongest defense for their actions, in the opinion of the entrepreneurs, and probably in that of much of the pub-lic, was that business was responsible for the development of the country, and that this was America's most important task.[38] Such an attitude helps to explain why Fish could think that the Interstate Commerce Act might function reasonably well, whereas the Chicago, Burlington and Quincy's Perkins thought it economically impossible; why the Louisville and Nashville's Smith favored competition as the basis for efficient business, but the Chicago, Burlington and Quincy's Harris thought it deadly to railroads.

---

[37]Cochran, p. 201.

[38]Ibid., p. 200.

III. ORGANIZATIONAL STRUCTURE

	1870	1880	1890	1900
A T & S F	Average	Average	Average	Average
B & M	Average	Average	Average	Average
C B & Q	Harmful	Superior	Superior	Superior
I C	Average	Average	Average	Average
L & N	Average	Harmful	Average	Average

Organizational design and the structuring of activities is pivotal to the success of large scale organizations. The effectiveness with which management dealt with the structuring process of the five railroads is perhaps best demonstrated by the following two major illustrations from the Louisville and Nashville and the Chicago, Burlington and Quincy.

The expansionary programs and competition of the 1870s brought administrative challenge. The five roads in question, although large by 1860 and 1870 standards, became huge systems between 1880 and 1900 by purchases, mergers, or new construction. Such growth necessitated revised, revamped, or totally new structuring and designs.

Although the Chicago, Burlington and Quincy experienced traffic and revenue increases in the post-war decade, revenues did not keep pace with traffic. In fact, as Overton notes, "average revenues per ton mile and per passenger mile fell steadily because of intensive competition. And, as rates fell, competition simply became sharper as greater efforts were made to increase traffic volume."[39] As a result,

---

[39]Overton, p. 108.

the post-war decade was characterized by competitive warfare interspersed with temporary truces and alliances that called for an organizational structure contingent upon environmental conditions.

From the standpoint of organization, the Chicago, Burlington and Quincy was ill-equipped to act in a unified or decisive manner. At the beginning of 1870, for example, the Chicago, Burlington and Quincy proper operated only in the state of Illinois. Various branch lines were operated separately. It is true that various members of the Forbes group[40] controlled the several companies through stock ownership. When it came to competing with the Rock Island or the North Western, all the Burlington family lines could be expected to act together.[41] But in bidding for traffic from the Union Pacific, one of the branch lines would automatically become a competitor of another. As Overton notes, "Harmony was lacking within the Burlington family itself."[42]

Had there been a chief executive officer for the entire system, some uniformity of policy might have resulted. But Joy, who most nearly occupied that position, was financially more interested in some lines than in others. As of 1870, for example, he was president of the Chicago, Burlington and Quincy and the Council Bluffs, and was the chief influence on the Hannibal. Brooks, meanwhile, was president of

---

[40]Overton uses the term "Forbes Group" to denote the fact that a number of individuals collectively formed a cohesive body of leadership talents. For example, Forbes was a mobilizer of capital; Joy, an astute lawyer; Brooks, an energetic operating man; and others as warranted.

[41]Overton, p. 108.

[42]Ibid.

the Burlington and Missouri of Iowa and also, in a few years, the Burlington and Missouri in Nebraska. Perkins was concerned exclusively with the welfare of the Iowa line, and Superintendent Harris of the Chicago, Burlington and Quincy was inclined to think only in terms of his particular road. Effective organization was lacking in the Burlington system in 1870.

In March 1880, Forbes was re-elected president of the Chicago, Burlington and Quincy. In order to provide adequate administrative supervision for the enlarged system, the directors separated the offices of vice-president and general manager and created two general manager positions. One was for all roads east of the Missouri, the other for those west of it, an organizational pattern that remains to this day.[43] This administrative reorganization with Forbes in the east and Perkins in the west marked the end of the first structural change and helped achieve harmony. With Perkins' election to president in 1881 he was destined to serve in that capacity for almost twenty years, longer than anyone else in the history of the system.

Perkins was expected to initiate and formulate policy and did so. In fact "it is probably correct to say that Perkins actually exercized more power than any other Burlington president before or since."[44] He streamlined the structure yet allowed and encouraged necessary refinement. For example, he believed strongly in delegation of responsibility and expected the men under him to use imagination and initiative in attaining the ultimate goal.

---

[43]Ibid., p. 171.

[44]Ibid., pp. 202-203.

Throughout his administration, Perkins never abandoned his efforts
to adapt the top managerial staff to the tasks confronting the railroad.[45] Thus, the Chicago, Burlington and Quincy was regarded as a
training ground for rail executives. For example, one of Perkins'
vice-presidents, W. B. Strong, became president of the Atchison,
Topeka and Santa Fe during the 1880s and E. P. Ripley, general freight
agent for the Chicago, Burlington and Quincy during the mid-1880s, was
destined to become president of the Atchison, Topeka and Santa Fe in
1895.

By the mid-1890s the financial and corporate structure of the
Chicago, Burlington and Quincy was quite complex. The existence of
numerous independent companies required substantive records and made
it a difficult if not nearly impossible task to calculate exactly how
the entire system was functioning. "Corporate simplification was im-
perative" and 'Perkins devoted great thought to the sort of financing
and structuring that would be best suited to these various ends.'[46]
He was successful, for "at the turn of the century the bewildering,
corporate structure of the Burlington was greatly simplified."[47] In
many ways, Perkins' achievement of the corporate and financial stream-
lining of the Chicago, Burlington and Quincy System by the turn of the
century was like putting the final touches on a castle under construction for years.

Perkins had, even before becoming president, "acquired the habit

----

[45]Ibid., p. 177.

[46]Ibid., p. 245.

[47]Ibid.

of writing extensive memoranda on every facet of railroading."[48] One
of these documents is especially noteworthy where it speaks of "Organization of Railroads."[49] Perkins based his comments on his experience
in reorganizing the administrative structure of the Chicago, Burlington
and Quincy. The road had developed a divisional structure with clear-
cut line and staff distinctions. Yet, because of Perkins' concern for
decentralization, it did not have a separate traffic department. Instead, the Chicago, Burlington and Quincy's traffic executives worked
within its several autonomous units. As Chandler relates in discuss-
ing Perkins' writing, "No better analysis exists of the organization of
a large railroad system and the needs that brought it into being."[50]

The Louisville and Nashville's development of organizational
structure and design evolved "more or less piecemeal,"[51] much as other
roads did during periods of rapid change and growth. The Louisville
and Nashville experienced continued growth over the years 1870, 1880,
1890, and 1900. Continued growth, however, brought not only more employees but also an increasingly complex structure of relationships
within the company. The evolving environment affected both internal
and external relationships. The responses by two officials--Fink and
Smith--help illustrate how the Louisville and Nashville chose to re-

---

[48]Ibid., p. 177.

[49]A memorandum of Charles E. Perkins, "Organization of Railroads"
(1885), published in Alfred D. Chandler, Jr., The Railroads: The
Nation's First Big Business (New York: Harcourt, Brace & World, Inc.
1965), pp. 118-125.

[50]Chandler, p. 100.

[51]Klein, p. 149.

act to structural and design issues.

The election of H. D. Newcomb as president of the Louisville and Nashville in 1870 was contingent upon his agreeing not to hold any executive office in another corporation. The board recognized that the Louisville and Nashville was entering a new era. Success had spawned rapid growth which in turn had produced an increasingly complex organization. Two obvious developments illustrated this trend -- the increase of personnel in every department and the growing specialization of function at every level.[52] The campaign of 1870 also witnessed the election of Albert Fink into a new position as second vice president.

The creation of Fink's new position testified to the need for more administrative officers. Although he continued to hold his post of general superintendent, his duties now evolved around policy matters. Slowly but surely a distinction between line and staff was emerging. As the amount and range of responsibility grew, the once fluid and informal administration of the Louisville and Nashville gradually became bureaucratized.[53] Fink was instrumental in developing policy issued in this area, however perhaps one of his major contributions was in the development and use of modern cost accounting.[54]

In addition to the Louisville and Nashville's concerns for expansion in 1870 and later were also those of competition. This brought a new emphasis to the task of administration. Cost analysis or cost accounting became important in the determination of cost and

[52]Ibid., p. 100.

[53]Ibid.

[54]Annual Report of the Louisville & Nashville Railroad Company for the year Ending June 30, 1874 (Louisville, 1874), pp. 37-47, 63-64.

therefore in the determination of profits and rate making. Such analysis also came to be used as an "effective way to evaluate the performance of operating executives."[55] The type of cost data developed by Fink helped make possible the "control through statistics" that has become an essential hallmark of modern corporate structures. Fink's landmark work did much to allow the Louisville and Nashville to get a better "handle" on where they stood and enabled decision-makers to make decisions based upon more complete data. This type of thinking led Fink's exposition to be labeled the "foundation stone of American railway economics."[56]

The accession of Milton H. Smith to the presidency of the Louisville and Nashville in 1884 marked the beginning of an administration that was to run until 1921. This led Klein to write, "During that long reign Smith influenced the course of the system's destiny more than any other man in its history except Albert Fink."[57] It was Smith "who did much to rationalize the Louisville and Nashville's administration into a cohesive structure capable of dealing with the complex problems" and who "helped shape the very kind of efficient, rational bureaucracy he was supposed to have resented."[58]

In the end Smith failed to erect his bureaucracy without bureaucrats. Slowly but surely the Louisville and Nashville's organizational structure grew in complexity. However, as long as Smith was in command

---

[55]Chandler, p. 99.

[56]Ibid., p. 100.

[57]Klein, p. 223.

[58]Ibid., p. 224.

his "personalized" manner of structuring would create resistence to the "depersonalized" aspects of large-scale bureaucracies.

As suggested above, there was irony in that most people today would view "bureaucracy" as inefficient and irrational, however, Smith subscribed more to Weberian ideology. Smith was devoted to efficiency, which meant he did not oppose bureaucracy itself but rather clumsy, cumbersome and inefficient bureaucracy. "Bureaucracy may be carried to such an extent," he observed, "the administration of the company's affairs may be so subdivided--as to render operations ineffective, resulting in at least partial paralysis."[59]

Adhering to these principles, Smith managed to keep the structure of his administration comparatively simple and streamlined. In point of reference Klein posits that "Smith built for the Louisville and Nashville an operating staff structure different from and simpler than that used by most railroad companies of comparable size" and in that sense justly earned the reputation of fostering a "personalized management at a time when corporations were becoming increasingly bureaucratized and their officers anonymous to the general public."[60]

Reasons such as the above demonstrate Smith's concern with the proliferation of departments. When, for example, the board recommended that an insurance department be created to handle all matters

---

[59]Starting with the pioneering work of German sociologist Max Weber, there has been a search for the ideal organizational structure. Weber called his ideal a bureaucracy. See A. M. Henderson and Talcott Parsons (trans. & eds.), Max Weber: The Theory of Social and Economic Organization (New York: Free Press, 1947).

[60]Klein, pp. 233-235.

in that area, Smith strongly opposed it--in fact in some ways antici-
pating Parkinson's law. He emphasized that "the tendency to waste and
extravagance" would be quite strong with the creating of bureaus which
would necessarily involve the creation of petty officers. Those
officers, he insisted, would soon unduly imagine themselves quite important, demanding greater remuneration, perquisites, and recognition
without any increased efficiency or productivity.[61]

IV. EXECUTIVE ABILITY

	1870	1880	1890	1900
A T & S F	Superior	Average	Harmful	Superior
B & M	Superior	Superior	Harmful	Superior
C B & Q	Superior	Superior	Superior	Superior
I C	Average	Average	Superior	Average
L & N	Superior	Average	Average	Average

General histories and textbooks often give the reader the im-
pression that anyone could have managed the early railroads and that
railroad practices were only an accumulation of experiences.[62] Actually "there were few precedents to guide those groping to devise
rational ways to supervise, coordinate, and plan for the use of far
more men, money, and equipment than any other private enterprise had

---

[61]Smith to Belmont, December 13, 1894, quoted at length in Klein,
pp. 234-235.

[62]Charles J. Kennedy, "The Early History of Four Massachusetts Railroads," reprinted from the Bulletin of the Business Historical
Society, XXV (March-December, 1959), p. 1. This paper will be included in the author's Railroad History: Entrepreneurial and Managerial Appraisal and Other Essays.

hitherto had to administer."[63] Thus, executive ability appears critical. In fact, as noted in Chapter IV, this category may be considered
the most important of the eleven divisions of the preliminary management audit because the quality of performance in the other ten depends upon the thinking and actions of the executive group. The executive talents of each of the five roads as a whole was about average for
the four years of 1870, 1880, 1890, and 1900. For example the
Atchison, Topeka and Santa Fe had its Strongs and Ripleys; the Boston
and Maine its Tuttle with some offset by Jones; the Chicago, Burlington
and Quincy its Joys, Forbes, and Perkins; the Illinois Central its
Ackermans and Fishs; and the Louisville and Nashville its Newcombs and
Smiths. Appendix F notes all of the railroad presidents from the
roads' inceptions through 1900.

Charles E. Perkins, only forty when elected president of the
Chicago, Burlington and Quincy, was destined to serve as president for
almost twenty years, longer than anyone else in the system. As Overton
notes, "it is probably correct to say that Perkins actually exercised
more power than any other Burlington president before or since."[64]

Perkins developed a habit of writing memoranda even before becoming president. He seemed challenged by the possibility of applying the
principles of scientific management to railroading before they were

---

[63]Alfred D. Chandler, Jr., "The Railroads: Pioneers in Modern
Corporate Management," Business History Review, XXXIX (1965), p. 16.

[64]Overton, p. 177.

generally accepted.[65] His usual approach was to establish general propositions (which he designated "natural laws"), and then demonstrate how they applied to the specific problem at hand.[66] But whereas he noted general principles, he recognized that in applying them, enough flexibility had to be allowed to meet specific situations at hand.

Perkins' contribution to administrative organization is also pivotal. He observed that the most important decisions on the road related to the traffic it had to carry. Second in rank were decisions relating to maintenance. He made another primary distinction regarding these two points as traffic increased by noting that scientific methods which would be "unnecessary and extravagant" on a new line would become "necessary and economical" on an established one.[67] The organization of an ever increasing system became increasingly complex.[68] Here Perkins visualized three vice-presidents to assist the chief executive--one for expenditures, negotiations, reports, and in particular "new schemes;" another for accounting and finances; and a third for operations with a general manager and purchasing agent reporting to him. The general manager in turn should have a general

---

[65]Frederick W. Taylor is usually considered the "father of scientific management." Perkins predated Taylor's published work of the early 1900 s although in all fairness to Taylor his ideas and thoughts were ruminating in the late 1800 s. See Frederick W. Taylor, The Principles of Scientific Management (New York: Harper, 1911).

[66]Overton, p. 177.

[67]Ibid., p. 178.

[68]This section leans heavily upon a memorandum of Perkins, "Organization of Railroads," written in 1885 and published in Alfred D. Chandler, Jr., The Railroads, pp. 118-125.

superintendent reporting to him, and if the road was large enough
it should have several divisions. As Cochran notes, "he appears to
have been among the first to understand the utility of titles to clarify
intermediate hierarchical positions, give their holders proper authority, and stimulate energy by a type of reward that "adds nothing to
the expenses."[69] Chandler's analysis of Perkins' organizational skills
is evidenced by noting 'no better analysis exists of the organization
of a large railroad system and the needs that brought it into being."[70]

No less important to Perkins than organization was the area of
labor relations. In this respect, he felt two factors were essential:
that proper personal influence be exerted by good officers and that a
strictly business relation be maintained between the corporation and
its employees. Accordingly, each employee should feel that he was
receiving a reasonable return for his labor and had a chance for promotion; and that each man should be treated by his superiors with "that
personal respect which is due from one man of proper feeling to
another."[71] He recognized fully that any individual was entitled to
his own private opinions, but he believed that "every man who works
for a railroad company is nevertheless bound to carry out its policy
in matters where it has a policy, and to do this in good faith and re-

---

[69]Cochran, p. 85.

[70]Chandler, The Railroads, p. 100.

[71]Overton, p. 179.

gardless of private opinions.[72]   Such illustrations justify Perkins
as a professional railroader.

A case in contrast is noted between the "professional railroader"
Perkins and the Illinois Central's "financier" Stuyvesant Fish.   President of the Illinois Central from 1887 to 1906, Fish's experience and
expertise was in financial and fiscal management and administration.
Not quite twenty-six when he became a director and five weeks shy of
being thirty-six when elected the president, he "never really had any
real experience in actual railroad operation."[73]   His eleven years
with the Illinois Central prior to 1887 had been in positions exclusively administrative and financial in nature.[74]

There was a difference between Fish, the financier, and his pred-
ecessor James Clarke, a railroad career man.   In fact, Cochran notes a
"striking contrast" not only between Clarke and Fish but "for that
matter between Fish and any of the Illinois Central presidents since
William Osborn."[75]   Fish, as Stover relates, was an "aristocrat" with
an ancestry that could be traced far back into the early history of
New York.[76]   He was a direct descendent of Peter Stuyvesant, the last
Dutch governor of New Amsterdam.   His grandfather was Colonel

---

[72]Perkins to Potter, January 1, 1885, and quoted in Cochran, p. 85.

[73]John F. Stover, History of the Illinois Central (New York: Alfred
A. Knopf, 1965), p. 210.

[74]Cochran, p. 317.

[75]Ibid., p. 46.

[76]Stover, p. 244.

Nickolas Fish, Revolutionary War soldier and lifelong friend of
Alexander Hamilton. And his father was Hamilton Fish, New York con-
gressman, governor, senator, and secretary of state in the cabinet of
Ulysses S. Grant. He attended Columbia University and earned his M.A.

Between 1877 and 1885 a new financial group had come to power in
the Illinois Central, composed of New York financiers such as the
Astors, Belmonts, and Morton, Bliss and Company--the new group which
made Fish president and Edward H. Harriman vice-president.[77] The influence of Harriman's financial holdings of the Illinois Central eventually were to be the demise of Fish, however it is difficult to write
of Fish without considering Harriman. In fact, Stover calls this
period of Illinois Central history the Harriman-Fish years.[78] During
Fish's tenure therefore, the presidency shifted from Chicago to New
York. Although "he always remained essentially a New York financial
man while General Manager Edward T. Jeffery ran operations until 1899,
Fish's scrutiny of affairs was close and his administration a strong
one."[79]

The nineteen year tenure of Fish presents formidable results. In
fact, the Illinois Central system expanded in nearly every way.
Illinois Central mileage more than doubled while both annual revenues
and the capital invested more than quadrupled. In financial prestige
the rating of the Illinois Central was among the best of American lines.

---

[77]Cochran, p. 46.

[78]Stover, pp. 206-242.

[79]Cochran, p. 47.

When Fish presided at the Illinois Central's golden anniversary banquet on February 9, 1901, he was able to announce that "for the first time in decades the majority of Illinois Central capital stock was owned by Americans rather than foreigners," and that there had been "a continuous policy of dividend payments."[80] Such results were envious; however, what of Fish's beliefs and attitudes?

One series of illustrations of Fish's ethics and honesty in regard to the public is enlightening. He held that neither he nor the Illinois Central could "afford to lose our good name, or be mixed up in a stock jobbing, bond stealing operation."[81] Regarding news interviews or letters as a means of planting opinion, Fish thought "that, as a general proposition, it is unwise for railroad officers to get themselves interviewed....It is better to put what they have to say into formal official communications.[82] Thus, he sent a reporter of the New York Tribune a letter "signed as from a correspondent in New Orleans.'[83] Regarding political payola, Fish wrote it was "wrong as a matter of principle and also as a matter of economy to pay for legislation," although he was willing to do so if "it cannot be obtained in any

---

[80]Stover, p. 207.

[81]Fish to W. Knight, president, Dubuque & Sioux City Railroad, January 28, 1888, and quoted in Cochran, p. 214.

[82]Fish to E. Jeffery, general manager, October 27, 1888, and quoted in Cochran, p. 186.

[83]Fish to J. C. Clarke, then president of Illinois Central, January 10, 1885, and quoted in Cochran, p. 186.

other way."[84] The implied philosophy seems to have been that sound
business was supported by higher sanction than that against influenc-
ing corrupt and incompetent legislators.

When Edward P. Ripley took charge of the Atchison, Topeka and
Santa Fe in late 1895, he inherited a road in receivership with a formidable managerial challenge. Ripley "worked a virtual miracle" however, and made the Santa Fe "one of the most profitable carriers in the
nation."[85] It had gotten into a sorry position because of overexpan-
sion, extravagances in operations, and an overly generous income in
dividends. [86] The credibility of the previous administration also had
become suspect, although perhaps unintentionally.[87] Ripley on the
other hand used Annual Reports, newspapers, magazines, public conferences and railroad regulatory hearings to carry his message to the
public.[88]

The Ripley management team proceeded cautiously in the years
following receivership. Changes in policy were carefully analyzed before decisions were made. Emphasis was shifted from construction and
acquisition to the enlargement of traffic on a paying basis. President
Ripley, an operations expert, was determined to develop and follow "a

---

[84]Fish to J. C. Clarke (then president of Illinois Central), March 13,
1885, and quoted in Cochran, p. 194.

[85]Bryant, pp. 182 and 200.

[86]Ibid., p. 153.

[87]London Economist quoted in James Marshall, Santa Fe: The Railroad
That Built an Empire (New York: Random House, 1945), p. 246.

[88]Bryant, p. 207.

model business program."[89] This was especially important because the difficulties of preceding years had centered public attention on the efforts to restore good will and respectability. As a recent student of the Ripley management has observed:

> It was in the executive offices of the Santa Fe Railroad in Chicago that one would find the emerging leadership of American railroads in this new era of professional manager-ship. This rapidly expanding railroad was playing a leading role in the fast-growing Southwest.[90]

Ripley spent virtually his entire life in the railroad industry. He joined the Chicago, Burlington and Quincy in 1870, becoming the New England agent, and by 1888 became general manager. After eighteen months he resigned to accept the position of third vice-president with the Chicago, Milwaukee and St. Paul Railway. His "reputation for honesty and integrity and his managerial skills" attracted the attention of J. P. Morgan and Company which "promoted his candidacy for the presidency" of the Atchison, Topeka and Santa Fe.[91] Ripley selected his lieutenants with great skill.

The dominant personality of Ripley, affectionately known by his employees as "the old man," was supplemented by the business acumen of his associates. Aldace Walker, the chairman of the Board, "had a shrewd eye for future traffic. Victor Morawetz, the general counsel...

---

[89]Waters, p. 342.

[90]Martin, p. 169.

[91]Bryant, p. 169.

contributed a solid background in corporate finance and relations with regulatory agencies." Paul Morton, the vice-president, supplied operational efficiency through his bureaucratic skills.[92] Ripley delegated considerable authority to his management team and soon created a positive atmosphere.

Ripley was a firm believer in _laissez-faire_, and desired limited rate-making by regulatory agencies, and rejected any role for labor unions in employees' relations. A "progressive" writer of the period found his views "medieval" on public questions,[93] but a more recent defender of the American railroad system argues that Ripley saw the growing problems of the industry long before other railroad executives perceived them.[94]

Ripley's outspokenness and bluntness sometimes caused unfavorable publicity, as in the case of the famous quote on tariff rates, "what the traffic will bear," taken out of context. Such candor was part of Ripley. He fought for the Atchison, Topeka and Santa Fe and the industry with tenacity, honesty, and blunt language, and was one of the industry's brilliant professional managers.

The Louisville and Nashville had its share of individuals with exemplary managerial ability. However, Milton H. Smith would most close-

[92]Ibid., p. 183.

[93]Albert Atwood, "Sound Properties: The Atchison," _Harper's Weekly_, LIX (July 18, 1914), p. 71.

[94]Martin, pp. 128-130.

ly approximate Ripley as a professional manager who took control under similar circumstances. The Louisville and Nashville's exuberant expansion program of the early 1880's created a substantial increase in the funded debt and a resulting increase in fixed charges. The climax came in the spring of 1884 with the financial scandal of then president C. C. Baldwin. Baldwin resigned under fire and his directors admitted that some wrongdoing had occurred.[95] In October, 1884, Milton H. Smith of Louisville became the president and was the dominant personality in the road to the year of his death, 1921. In Klein's book, The History of the Louisville and Nashville, chapter eleven is entitled "A Curmudgeon for All Seasons: Milton H. Smith and His Administration."[96] In dedication, single-mindedness of purpose, and "sheer tenacity, he was unrivaled."[97] The effect of his thirty seven year presidency was to create the legend that Milton H. Smith ran the Louisville and Nashville -- indeed that he was the Louisville and Nashville -- and that he represented a last bastion of rugged individualism in the corporate era.[98]

After assuming the presidency he warned sharply that "management must be sound to the core." He added that the dishonesty and criminal incompetency that pervaded the management of this property more or less

---

[95]Stover, The Railroads of the South, 1865-1900: A Study in Finance and Control (Chapel Hill: The University of North Carolina Press), p. 229.

[96]Klein, pp. 223-243.

[97]Ibid., p. 223.

[98]Ibid., p. 223.

from 1875 to 1884 could obtain in the future without disaster.[99] He
took firm control. His rigid retrenchment -- a ten percent reduction
in all administrative and clerical salaries, a twenty percent reduction in the workforce of all non-operating departments, and a cur-
tailment in passenger and legal expenses -- was a step toward the
restoration of sound principles of management. He was a railroad man
who became 'more personally identified with his company than virtually
any other railroad men of his era."[100]

The next category explores the role of the board of directors and
what more fitting analysis than to illustrate Smith's "stern managerial
genius" with the Louisville and Nashville Board?

V. DIRECTORATE EFFECTIVENESS

	1870	1880	1890	1900
A T & S F	Average	Superior	Average	Average
B & M	Superior	Average	Average	Average
C B & Q	Average	Average	Average	Average
IC	Average	Average	Average	Average
L & N	Harmful	Average	Average	Superior

In the world of proprietorships, partnerships and small business,
the right to control the organization has been associated with owner-
ships. The growth of large scale corporate organization with widespread ownership created the need for new relationships between manage-

---

[99] Smith to Directors, September 14, 1885, as quoted in Klein,
   p. 222.

[100] Ibid., p. 235.

ment, boards, and stockholders. This raised the problem of "who represented the absentee owners, who could wield the ultimate power, or who was the most important in prescribing the executive role."[101] On most of the roads studied, this question can be answered rather pragmatically by those individuals who as presidents had substantial investment in the particular organization or those who could muster enough of the stockholder's ballots at elections.

Forbes, for example, after gaining control of the Chicago, Burlington and Quincy board in a proxy battle at a time when he held only a moderate amount of stock, recognized both his power and obligations: "I have no doubt we can now have our own way on all reasonable things, and you know I never want any other . . . . with victory will, I fear, come responsibility and care. It would have been far easier just to have stepped out and sold my stock, and had an easy life; and I expect to repent not doing so."[102]

As suggested in the last category--executive ability--Smith of the Louisville and Nashville assumed that basic strategic decisions were essentially in his domain. If the course he decided upon cost money, it was up to the financial genius of the board to supply it. As Mary Tachau put it, "His relationship with his boards was essentially a _foedus_ _inter_ _pares_: They were to provide a sound and adequate

---

[101]Cochran, p. 62.

[102]Forbes, to a member of the family, February 28, 1875, as quoted in Henry G. Pearson, An American Railroad Builder: John Murray Forbes (New York, Arno, 1972), p. 178.

financial base, and he would protect their property."[103] Implicit in Smith's argument was the belief that all were working for the same objective; yet, this was not always the case. Both Smith and his boards were vitally interested in the Louisville and Nashville but from different vantage points. Smith believed the system and its needs were paramount and that profits should be plowed back, whereas the board reasoned that "if Smith were allowed a free rein, the Louisville and Nashville might prosper and flourish but the stockholders would pay for the success with no income."[104] The board, however, controlled finances and exerted its influence as the following illustrates.

After resuming the presidency of the Louisville and Nashville in 1891, Smith renewed his argument that he was in a better position to understand the company's needs and should therefore have the final word on important strategy questions.[105] To Smith's assertion, board member Jacob H. Schiff replied that the board maintained that although

> The efficient management of the company's affairs must originate with the president...the proprietors, whose representation is in the first instance concentrated in the chairman of the board, must have a right to review and determine every important question connected with the management of the company's affairs. ...therefore,...the chairman shall.../not be restricted solely7 to the finances of the company.[106]

---

[103]Mary K. Bonsteel Tachau, "The Making of a Railroad President: Milton Hannibal Smith and the Louisville and Nashville," _Filson Club History Quarterly_, XLIII, No. 2 (April, 1969), p. 129.

[104]Klein, p. 246.

[105]Ibid., p. 242.

[106]Cyrus Alder, _Jacob H. Schiff: His Life and Letters_ (New York: Doubleday, Doran, 1929), p. 59.

Such a statement is a succint indication of the role of the board and
the limitations of Smith's authority. Smith may have been the Louisville and Nashville, but he could not determine everything. At a
higher plain, one might argue that such conflicts between Smith and
the board represented signs of a gradually emerging corporate maturity.
If conflict arose between the president and the board what of conflicts within the board itself?

In the Louisville and Nashville elections of 1871, tensions over
expansion, rates and policy issues found directors "hopelessly irrec-
oncilable:"

> Unable to satisfy every interest of the community, they
> could no longer function comfortably in the dual roles
> of director and customer, stockholder and shipper...it
> was plain...that the friction lay not between the corpor-
> ation and the community but between equally ambitious
> interest groups with differing goals.[107]

In each of the five railroads in this study, the leading directors often took active roles. This, incidentally, is in contrast to
Drucker's view of the "withering away" of the board as being inherent
in the structure of corporate enterprise.[108] The active role taken by
the Atchison, Topeka and Santa Fe board is demonstrated in Bradley's

---

[107]Klein, p. 98.

[108]Peter F. Drucker, The New Society (New York: Harper, 1950), p. 223.
As Robert A. Gordon, Business Leadership In the Large Corporation
(Washington: Brookings Institute, 1945), p. 144, says: "Boards of
Directors as formal bodies do not exercise a significant degree of
active leadership in most large corporations. There is no question
that initiation of decisions comes from the executive group rather
than from the board. The latter's failure to initiate decisions or
to formulate policies is less significant than the fact that
directors have largely yielded their approval to the group of
officials whom in theory they are supposed to supervise."

treatise in his discussion of the road's acquisition of the Southern
Kansas Railroad on December 16, 1880. He stated that "the Santa Fe
directors themselves, made this acquisition largely for self-pro-
tection of their corporation." Further, they "believed, incidentally,
that the Southern Kansas under good management would prove a valuable
property, and in this they were fully justified."[109]

Boards acted at times without much regard for the operating executive's opinion or even for the necessity of informing him.[110] The
directors of the Illinois Central, dominated first by the strong personality of William Osborn and later by powerful banking interests,
were inclined to act on occasion without much regard for the opinion
of the president.[111] It would appear that both presidents Douglas and
Ackerman complained strongly about actions taken by their boards without consulting them. President Ackerman, for example, had to seek information regarding board action on his immediate subordinates. "Is
the office of General Manager abolished," he asked, "and do the duties
of that office devolve upon the General Superintendent?" In correspondence with his treasurer, Ackerman complained, "Would it not be
safer to refer matters regarding traffic arrangements to this office

---

[109]Glenn Danford Bradley, The Story of the Santa Fe (Boston: Gorham Press, 1920), p. 230. Underlining added.

[110]Cochran, p. 67.

[111]Ibid.

before action is taken by the board?"[112] That these troubles were not
due to special distrust of either Douglas's or Ackerman's judgment or
to Osborn as an individual is indicated by their continuance during
Clarke's administration under the banker regime.[113]

Discussion of the ideas of the early managements and boards of the
five roads on the emerging roles of stockholders, directors and managers indicates that the growth of managerial power was inherent in the
developments of large scale corporations. But the emergence of what
Oswald Knuth called the "managerial enterprise" was impeded (1) by the
traditional language and employee rates carried over from proprietory
ventures, (2) by the presence of powerful general entrepreneurs on the
board, and (3) by the perpetration of the general entrepreneurial
power through investment bankers.[114] As long as the "general entrepreneurs" remained personally active, it could not be said that the
"captain of industry was succeeded by an officialdom whose members
held each his office-in-trust, his realm of discretion and responsibility."[115]

Financial prowess was a concern for stockholders, directors and
managers as well. In fact, fiscal policy issues were pivotal in
management performance. The managerial ability of the five railroads

[112]Ackerman, President, to Randolph, Treasurer, December 26, 1876:
Ackerman, President, to Randolph, Treasurer, February 13, 1878; and
Douglas, President, to Osborn, Director, March 9, 1867, as quoted
in Cochran, p. 67.

[113]Cochran, p. 67.

[114]Oswald Knuth, Managerial Enterprise (New York: Norton, 1948).

[115]Walton H. Hamilton and Irene Till, "Property," Encyclopedia of
Social Sciences, 1934.

in that aspect, given environmental circumstances is explored next.

VI. FISCAL POLICY

	1870	1880	1890	1900
A T & S F	Average	Average	Harmful	Superior
B & M	Average	Average	Harmful	Average
C B & Q	Average	Average	Average	Average
I C	Average	Harmful	Average	Average
L & N	Harmful	Average	Average	Superior

This category is concerned with management's providing, controlling and husbanding of capital. As noted in Chapter IV, the objective of sound fiscal policy is to conserve, employ, and account for the resources of the organization so that funds are available when needed to achieve the organization's short and long range goals. This category, then, will explore through selected illustrations how various managements developed their roads' financial policy.

The financial policy of early railroads was fraught with risks and difficulties. Relatively new corporations offered prospects for financial rewards and likewise possibilities of loss. Local funds usually became inadequate to meet the needs of a capital intensive industry and promoters had to amass large amounts of capital from distant locations. Thus financing and financial policy were developed under varying circumstances and resort was made to many methods.

Atchison Associates was formed in September 1868 to build the Atchison, Topeka and Santa Fe. This syndicate was able to raise funds through a questionable technique. Various issues were lumped

together and units prepared which contained small parcels in each.
The initial offering, dated 1869, included (a) $960,000 in par value
of common stock, (b) $150,000 in Shawnee County, Kansas bonds, (c)
$192,000 of first mortgage bonds of the Santa Fe, and (d) $768,500 of
Pottawatomie land bonds.[116] Although all of the bonds paid seven percent interest and the mortgage bonds had thirty-year maturities and
the land bonds ten years, only $955,700 in cash had been realized from
the $2,070,500 in securities marketed. In effect, the sales meant that
over half the securities were "watered." Thus, "the first financing
venture of the Santa Fe throws light on an interesting aspect of
watered stock . . . ."[117] After that action the Atchison Associates
terminated its contract with the Atchison, Topeka and Santa Fe and a
group of Bostonians took over the management.

This shift led to a fortuitous change, for Henry Keyes proved to
be an excellent president although he served only until September
1870. Keyes arranged for Kidder, Peabody and Company to become financial agents and for Baring Brothers of London to become the railroad's
European agents. Kidder, Peabody and Company's sales methods proved
to be much more successful than selling bonds with a stock bonus. The
degree of "watering" lessened as the company's stocks and bonds began
more nearly to represent actual assets. This conservative method of
financing became a hallmark of the Atchison, Topeka and Santa Fe for
many years. Ginery Twitchell, who succeeded Keyes as president in

---

116Henry V. Poor, Poor's Manual of the Railroads of the United States
(New York, 1870-1 to 1902). 1870.

117Waters, p. 180.

1870, "maintained the company's reputation of being shrewdly managed."[118]

At the outset of the 1880's, the second decade of Atchison, Topeka and Santa Fe operation, "the finances of the company," under the tutelage of T. J. Coolidge, "were in good order."[119] The year ending December 31, 1880, disclosed total assets of $51,940,657, of which $18,604,126 represented securities of subsidiaries.[120] Funded debt of $15,873,000 was less than two-thirds the capital stock account of $24,891,000. The ratio of debt to capital stock was "extremely conservative[121] and well within the limits laid down by principles of sound, conservative finance.[122] Interest charges average about seven percent and the coverage of fixed charges was in excess of the recommended figure of two. $3,022,410 was carried to the surplus account and quarterly dividends totaling seven and one half percent ($1,727,195) were declared. The showing was all the more impressive when consideration was given to the fact that one-half of the stock had been issued during the year and did not reflect full earning power in such a short period.[123] The surge of prosperity continued until

---

[118]Bryant, p. 19-20.

[119]Waters, p. 187.

[120]See Appendix C. Table C:1.

[121]Waters, p. 187.

[122]See, for example, John Moody, How to Analyze Railroad Reports (New York: Analyses Publishing Co., 1912).

[123]All of the new stock did not bring cash into the treasury, but the overall operations during the year were to increase the capitalization coincidentally by the amount of the stock. Of the increase in stock, $3,257,500 grew out of the conversion of consolidated

the recession of 1887. A reorganization, however, was necessary in
1889.

In the reorganization Allen Marvel was promoted to president in
place of Strong. Under the tutelage of Kidder, Peabody and Company,
a plan for voluntary financial reorganization was prepared. The objectives sought were a reduction in fixed charges, a consolidation of
various security issues, simplification of the corporate structure, and
funding of the floating debt.[124]

Financial results of operations after the reorganization were
mixed. For the year ending June 30, 1890, gross revenues were
$31,004,357 with net revenues of $10,083,971. The funded debt had
risen to $231,655,470 and the accumulated surplus had declined from
$8,049,700 in 1880 to $770,134 in 1890. The financial reorganization
of 1889 to all outward appearances seemed a success. What followed,
however, was a "catastropic decision in the annals of the Atchison,
Topeka and Santa Fe."[125]

In 1892, George C. Magoun, chairman of the board and J. W.
Reinhart, general auditor, decided that the time had come when prospects for earnings justified the refunding of the income bonds into
fixed-charge obligations. Thus, a total of $100,000,000 in second-
class mortgages was authorized. Converting a contingent charge into

---

mortgage bonds and $6,756,700 was issued in exchange for securities
of newly acquired lines. The remainder of $2,242,400 was marketed
to provide means of buying equipment. Two bond issues bearing
5 percent were floated to raise $4,916,000.

[124]Waters, p. 197.

[125]Waters, p. 204 and Bryant, pp. 123-152.

a fixed charge was extremely questionable in view of the fact that the Atchison, Topeka and Santa Fe had earned no more than the amount of the new fixed charges. It would be necessary for earnings to improve to enable the company to meet the obligations as they fell due.

When Marvel died during the next year, Reinhart became president. He enjoyed a reputation as a knowledgeable railroad accountant and financier. Even though Reinhart gave assurances that all was well, rumors of the impending insolvency of the Atchison, Topeka and Santa Fe soon were widespread.[126] The fixed charges became overburdening. Although Reinhart's actions precipitating the eventual reorganization had been debated, it would appear his financial plans were questionable and lacking in accuracy.[127]

Various plans were forwarded for reorganization. The final plan was the product of the joint executive committee of the board. It proposed to foreclose under the general mortgage and "to vest the properties acquired at foreclosure sale in a new company"[128] and to (1) reduce fixed charges to a safe limit, (2) provide for future capital requirements, (3) liquidate the floating debt and extinguish prior lien claims, (4) reinstate existing securities under equitable terms in their order of priority, (5) and unify the system in the interest of economy.[129] The financial plan of reorganization proved successful.

---

[126]Bryant, p. 150.

[127]Waters, pp. 206-217.

[128]Ibid., pp. 214-215.

[129]Ibid.

Under the new management of Edward F Ripley, improved earnings resulted and sound fiscal policy was established. Poor's Manual prefaced its surveys of the Atchison, Topeka and Santa Fe with the remark that "the company's capitalization is a model among railroads."[130] Waters noted that "under the presidency of Ripley the operations... were conducted on the highest plane of business ethics. The interlude of dark days was gone.... The Santa Fe waxed rich in public esteem as receivership faded in the distance."[131]

VII. OPERATING EFFICIENCY

	1870	1880	1890	1900
A T & S F	Average	Average	Superior	Superior
B & M	Average	Average	Harmful	Average
C B & Q	Average	Average	Harmful	Average
I C	Average	Average	Average	Superior
L & N	Average	Harmful	Average	Average

The quality of management in this category is evidenced by the ability to utilize equipment effectively and to handle "manpower management" efficiently. There are a number of indicators of railroad operating efficiency used today by the Association of American Railroads.[132] Some of the items of data necessary to compute these ratios

---

[130]Poor's Manual.

[131]Waters, p. 217.

[132]Charles J. Kennedy, "Measuring the Operating Efficiency of Early American Railroads" (Lincoln, Nebraska: College of Business Administration, University of Nebraska - Lincoln, 1979), p. 7,

or indicators are available in some but not all of the railroad reports to the stockholders. A certain few state railroad committees or
commissions also asked for such data as ton-miles and train-miles.
With the advent of the Interstate Commerce Commission and its annual
Statistics of Railways in the United States beginning in 1888, all
railroads were required to report the information which Massachusetts
and a few other state legislatures had been requiring for several decades. Thus, for any railroad after 1887 one is able to compute the
following indicators:

> Average Freight Trainload in Tons
> Ton-miles per miles operated (Freight Traffic Density)
> Freight Revenue as a percent of Total Revenue.[133]

Also, the transportation ratio, one of the income accounts, can be
used with other data as an indicator of efficiency. (See column 11 in
Appendix C, below). That is, when there is no noticeable change in
the variable factors, such as (a) the amount of passenger service and
other income and (b) costs for train service, then noticeable changes
in the transportation ratio will indicate changes in operating efficiency. The so-called operating ratio (column 12), however, does not
measure operating efficiency unless all other variables in the income

---

listing the types of data used by J. Elmer Monroe of the A.A.R. in
Statement on the Railroad Financial Situation Before Presidential
Emergency Board Number 114, in the 1955 Non-operating Employees'
Wage Increase Case (Nov. 30, 1955), p. 56.

[133]See columns 17, 18, and 23 in Appendix C below for each of the
five railroads in this study.

statement remain stable, which is extremely unlikely.[134]

Figure 5:1, on the following page, illustrates the fluctuations of the operating ratio of the five railroads for each of the four years of 1870, 1880, 1890, and 1900. Figure 5:2 depicts the transportation ratio, or the cost of transporting passengers and freight, for each of the years 1870, 1880, 1890, and 1900 for the five roads.

The second major component of this category refers to "manpower management." All five of the roads experienced labor strikes of varying durations and thus were baptized into the growing complexity of management-labor relations. This occurred during periods of rapid change. Continued growth brought not only many more employees but also increasingly complex structures of relationships within the organizations. The evolving economic environment affected employees no less than it did management. Two examples, one from the Atchison, Topeka and Santa Fe and another from the Chicago, Burlington and Quincy will be briefly reviewed.

A wage dispute led to the first strike on the Atchison, Topeka and Santa Fe. In 1877 the management reduced wages five percent; later, conductors' salaries were cut from $120 to $75. The employees struck, but when management refused to restore the cuts, they returned to work for a lower wage. A second strike occurred in 1878 when engineers received a ten percent pay reduction. Feeling ran high and eventually the governor of Kansas called out the militia. The management hired

[134]Richard K. Darr, A History of the Nashua and Lowell Rail-Road Corporation 1835-1880 (New York: Arno Press, 1976), pp. 324-325. See also John Moody, How to Analyze Railroad Reports (New York: Analysis Publishing Company, 1912).

FIGURE 5:1

OPERATING RATIOS
OF
FIVE SELECTED RAILROADS

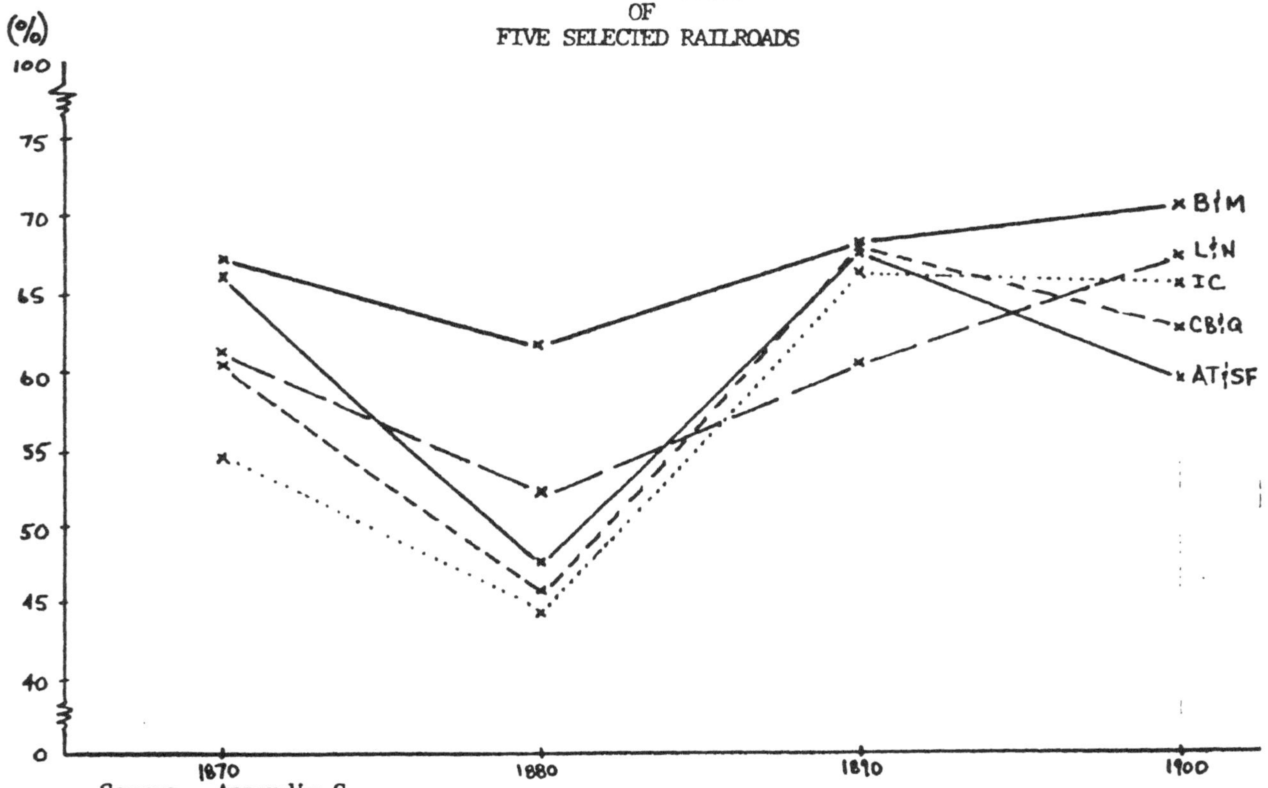

Source: Appendix C

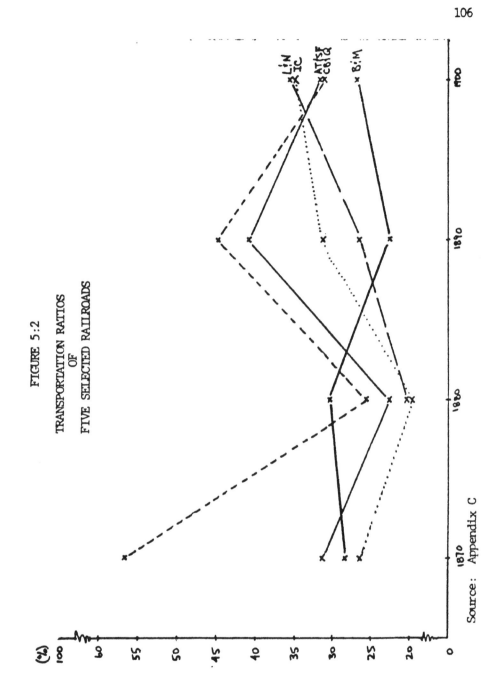

FIGURE 5:2

TRANSPORTATION RATIOS
OF
FIVE SELECTED RAILROADS

Source: Appendix C

replacements for the strikers and in its 1878 Annual Report denounced the "tramps and vagabonds" attracted by the strike.[135] The crisis passed, and according to Bryant "the management slowly realized that wage cuts were not conducive to good labor relations, and began to deal with labor problems in a less autocratic manner."[136] Under Strong's tutelage, however, workers were not allowed to dictate policy on wage or hours. Despite Strong's demands, the employees developed a sense of loyalty to both him and the company. Some employee benefits such as social insurance were provided, and Strong established a system of modest cash gratuities.[137] Programs such as these "were not done to forestall the organization of the employees; rather it was a part of a program of enlightened selfishness of the sort epitomized by Henry Ford's revolutionary wage scale of five dollars a day.[138]

Although the Atchison, Topeka and Santa Fe was not an "equal opportunity" employer, the first woman was hired in 1874. Various labor problems arose, such as in 1881 when eighteen section men were arrested for padding payrolls, but in total "the Atchison, Topeka and Santa Fe developed a reputation for fairness among the brotherhood of railway men."[139] This kind of thinking was shared by Waters in noting

---

[135]Bryant, p. 57.

[136]Ibid.

[137]Ibid.

[138]Waters, p. 286. See also Neal Owen Higgens, "The Early Pension Plans of the Baltimore and Ohio and the Pennsylvania Railroads 1880-1937" (Ph.D. Thesis, University of Nebraska Lincoln , 1974).

[139]Bryant, p. 57.

"through judicious and forthright administration the Santa Fe developed a family spirit and an intense loyalty on the part of its personnel."[140] Probably the regime of E. P. Ripley marked the climax of goodwill.

When the engineers on the Chicago, Burlington and Quincy struck in 1888, only a few Atchison, Topeka and Santa Fe employees went out sympathetically. Two years later, the Atchison, Topeka and Santa Fe management made substantial concessions to their trainmen; thereby raising its prestige as a reputable employer. The Trainmen's Journal commented: "the...agreement /was7...a valuable one, and the employees whose persistent and determined efforts secured it have good reason to be proud of their work. It is profitable to pay good wages to toilers...."[141] This agreement included a complicated dual basis of payment as well as seniority provisions. Detailed rules were agreed upon for overtime, turnarounds, and other points at issue. This action might have been profitably followed by other railroads. But what of the Chicago, Burlington and Quincy?

The strike of 1888, according to Overton, was "the most serious and significant labor conflict in the history of the Burlington."[142] The causes of the engineers' strike "on one of the largest, best-managed roads" in the nation is the subject of McMurry's authoritative account entitled The Great Burlington Strike of 1888.[143] The strike proved

---

140Waters, p. 286.

141Trainmen's Journal, Sept., 1890, as quoted in ibid., p. 314.

142Overton, p. 206.

143Donald L. McMurry, The Great Burlington Strike of 1888 (Cambridge, Harvard University Press, 195).

costly to both sides. The brotherhoods spent more than $1,500,000 in benefits and for publicity, and it cost the company probably twice that much. In fact, never again during Perkins' administration did dividends reach the pre-strike level. Forbes admitted that the conflict had retarded the expansion of the entire system.[144] Even so, according to Overton, "management felt that the financial sacrifice had been a sound investment, for to their thinking, the company had successfully reasserted its right to manage its own property."[145]

The issue of management's perogative to manage was strongly advocated by Perkins. In regard to labor relations it appears he felt two factors were essential: that proper personal influence be exerted by good officers and that a strictly business relation be maintained between the corporation and its employees. Accordingly, each employee should feel that he was receiving a reasonable return for his labor and had a chance for development and promotion; each employee should be treated by his supervisor with the personal respect which is due from one person to another.

Like Forbes, Perkins believed that managers should be developed to ensure future growth of the organization. Simply hiring the right employee was not enough. He said that it was up to every officer in a position of responsibility "to see that, in the ranks below him, men are growing up who can take the responsible places now filled by himself and others, and no officer is as good as he ought to be unless he

---

[144]Overton, p. 213.
[145]Ibid.

pays attention to duty, although it is neglected probably more than any other duty which is imposed upon railroad officials."[146] Attitudes and beliefs such as these were to ensure a steady supply of able management.

VIII. MARKETING EFFECTIVENESS

	1870	1880	1890	1900
A T & S F	Average	Superior	Superior	Average
B & M	Average	Average	Average	Average
C B & Q	Average	Superior	Superior	Average
I C	Superior	Average	Average	Average
L & N	Average	Average	Harmful	Average

It is the customer who determines what a business is or does, and the marketing concept necessitates meeting customer needs at a reasonable profit.[147] Because its purpose is to create a customer by meeting his needs at a profit, Drucker argues that "the business enterprise has two -- and only these two -- basic functions: marketing and innovation and that "all the rest are costs."[148]

Marketing is so basic that it cannot be considered entirely separate from the other categories as it overlaps and interrelates with all

---

[146]Perkins' "Promotion and Dismissal," 1883, as quoted in ibid., p. 181.

[147]The marketing concept places the consumer at the "hub" and necessitates the organization to meet his needs while at the same time recognizing the need to generate a profit. The marketing concept is the anti-thesis of the selling concept which puts the organization at the "hub" to provide those services it deems necessary with minimal concern for the customer.

[148]Drucker, Management, p. 61.

others. It is the whole railroad seen from the point of view of its final result, that is, from the customer's point of view. Therefore, several illustrations of marketing effectiveness are noted below.

Although all five of the railroads gained the majority if not all of their revenues from passenger or freight traffic in later years, the early years were marked with land sales. The Illinois Central's marketing of land grants typifies its early development of marketing strategy.

The business of the Illinois Central was not passively acquired. In reality much was created by the company as an outgrowth of a well-developed program of real estate development. In its real estate efforts the Illinois Central had two major objectives.[149] First, the company wished to gain a return from the land grants in order to re-deem and pay off the debt incurred as the charter lines were con-structed. Second, and more important, the company desired to settle the empty prairie lands adjacent to the railroad with stable farm families--settlers whose crops and varied needs would ensure a growing traffic for the new line.

Promotional activities took the form of pamphlets, circulars, newspapers, and various new techniques and innovations. President Osborn arranged to have advertising cards placed in visible spots in the horse streetcars serving several of the principal avenues in New York.[150] As Stover notes, "another innovation was the employment of

---

[149]Stover, Illinois Central, p. 108.

[150]Ibid., p. 117.

traveling agents to interest would-be land buyers in eastern and
southern states and also in Canada."[151]

A generous credit policy was also implemented by Illinois
Central's management; as the 1864 Annual Report notes, "the policy of
the /Land_7 Department has been liberal to the party actually settled
upon and working the land. Great care has been taken not to dis-
possess any man making an honest effort to work his farm, and this
course has established confidence in the company."[152] Most of the
land owned by the Illinois Central had been sold by 1870, and only
about half a million acres remained available.

The land selling efforts of later administrations of the Illinois
Central continued in the last three decades of the nineteenth century,
but at a slower pace. The Illinois Central "probably sold land to
about thirty five thousand different families in the second half of
the nineteenth century" and as Stover adds these land sales "clearly
played a significant role in the social and economic development" of
Illinois.[153]

Perhaps one of the most exemplary examples of marketing effectiveness is the relationship -- the working together -- of the
Atchison, Topeka and Santa Fe managements and Fred Harvey, purveyor
of fine food. Not only did Fred Harvey become one of the most powerful advertising media at the command of the Atchison, Topeka and
Santa Fe but social refinement and profitability were occasioned.

151Ibid., p. 117.

152Illinois Central, Annual Report (1864) p. 1.

153Stover, Illinois Central, p. 126.

Fred Harvey operated lunchrooms in Wallace, Kansas and Hugo, Colorado while he held the rank of General Western Agent of the Chicago, Burlington and Quincy. In the course of his travels he became convinced that the opportunity existed for a profitable operation if the right type of accommodations, food and service were offered. Attempts to induce the Chicago, Burlington and Quincy management to cooperate in establishing eating houses on their line were unsuccessful. Harvey then began negotiations with C. F. Morse of the Atchison, Topeka and Santa Fe and, after receiving approval of President Nickerson, obtained the rights. Harvey opened his Topeka lunch counter on the basis of a gentlemen's agreement. The arrangements called for the Atchison, Topeka and Santa Fe to supply the buildings and Harvey to equip them. Problems of joint concern were solved as soon as they were noticed. "Whatever is fair" was the guiding principle.[154]

Fred Harvey's contribution was considerable to both the Atchison, Topeka and Santa Fe, and to the eating habits and comforts of the population served.[155] His patrons learned what good food tasted like[156]

[154]Waters, p. 267.

[155]Harold L. Henderson, "Fredrick Henry Harvey," unpublished master's thesis, University of Kansas City, 1942), p. 19.

[156]As opposed to rancid, stale, tasteless food, a typical 75 cent Harvey menu might be: blue points on shell, whitefish with Madeira sauce, young capon with hollandaise sauce, roast beef, English-style baked veal pie, and prairie chicken accompanied by seven different vegetables, four salads--including lobster salad au mayonnaise--and a wide variety of pies, cakes and custards, followed by cheese and coffee. Even in an isolated town like Coolidge, Kansas, a Harvey customer could report that "Without a butcher, or grocer, or gardener, within hundreds of miles, here was an elegant supper, which might be said to have been brought from the ends of the earth and set down in the middle of the American desert." Noble R. Prentis, Southwestern Letters (Topeka Kansas: Kansas Publishing House, 1882), p. 34.

as well as quality service by Harvey "Girls."[157] Harvey, his managers
and his "girls," "civilized the west" by providing wholesome food
served in graceful style.[158]

Fred Harvey's operations definitely aided the management of the
Atchison, Topeka and Santa Fe. Labor-management relations eased as
crewmen on the line received excellent food and lodging, something
lacking on other railroads.[159] Passenger-traffic promotion benefited
from the reputation of "meals by Fred Harvey." In fact, when Nickerson
and Strong decided to make the Atchison, Topeka and Santa Fe a transcontinental railroad, they persuaded Harvey to follow the track gangs
to California.[160] Harvey restaurants served as "normal schools" for
the training of cooks, managers and waitresses. As one critic wrote

---

[157]As Bryant, p. 114-116 notes: About half of the Harvey employees
were men--the managers, chefs, buyers, and commissary superintendents; the female employees were largely the "Harvey Girls,"
the waitresses. The "Harvey Girls" came from "back East," particularly from the Midwest and New England, recruited by advertisements
in newspapers and young women's magazines. The Harvey matrons and
managers sought young women between eighteen and thirty years of age
who were attractive and intelligent. Recruiters tried to avoid
schoolteachers because the managers thought they were not suited to
the routine of the restaurants. The "girls" agreed to refrain from
marriage for one year, but the turnover rate remained high.
Dressed in black shoes and stockings, plain black dresses with an
"Elsie collar" and a black bow, and a heavily starched white apron,
their hair plainly done with a white ribbon, the "Harvey Girls"
stood in sharp contrast to the "painted ladies" of the nearby
saloons. Many of the "girls" were well educated, but all became
highly trained under the watchful eyes of the matrons, managers,
superintendents and Harvey, himself.

[158]Bryant, p. 113.

[159]Ibid., p. 116.

[160]Ibid.

shortly after Harvey's death, "Harvey eating-houses served as schools to all the southwest, bringing about a general reform. The rival railway systems and other competitive lunchrooms could no longer persevere in their barbarian ways."[161]

The Harvey services enhanced the passenger traffic of the Atchison, Topeka and Santa Fe for "with the close cooperation of Harvey and his sons, the executives of the Santa Fe made the railroad famous for its passenger service."[162] Presidents William B. Strong and Edward P. Ripley found in Fred Harvey a significant asset, and both the railroad and Harvey profited. This was not the case in Smith's attitude toward passenger service on the Louisville and Nashville. Not all events are examples of marketing effectiveness--of meeting customer needs, as the following illustration of the Louisville and Nashville's Smith depicts.

When Smith became president in the mid-1880s he found that the Louisville and Nashville lagged behind in demand for cars, although it was superior to most southern roads in the quantity and variety of its rolling stock. Part of the problem lay in the decrepit condition of the rolling stock inherited from acquired lines. For example, in 1887, the company added 14 locomotives and 779 new cars but condemned 11 engines and broke up 555 cars.[163] The financial squeeze, extension projects, acquisitions, economic depression and the

---

161Henry T. Fink, Food and Flavor (New York: The Century Co., 1913), p. 8.

162Bryant, p. 122.

163Klein, p. 330.

desirability of granting dividends all put pressures upon the Louisville and Nashville financial resources. With this confrontation
Smith had to assign priorities and funneled most of his resources into
motive power and freight cars. This policy by itself may have been
well conceived; however, his attitude toward passenger service was not.

Smith had never cared much for passenger business because as he
was reputed to have said, "You can't-make a g-- d----- cent out of
it."[164] Smith's statement was to haunt him in much the same fashion
that Vanderbilt's "public be damned" statement was to haunt him. The
result of Smith's marketing policy was that passenger business assumed
a progressively smaller proportion of the Louisville and Nashville's
business even though the revenues derived from it increased in
absolute terms (see Appendix C:5).

The Chicago, Burlington and Quincy's management may be cited for
its contribution to marketing effectiveness in various areas. Especially outstanding were the achievements of the Fast Mail and the promotional activities during Perkins' administration. The Fast Mail was
a mail train which ran from Chicago to Council Bluffs as part of a
mail service from New York to California.[165] The achievement of the
Fast Mail prompted Perkins to write Potter concerning suggestions for
advertising based upon repetition. Specifically, he thought the

---

164Quoted in John F. Stover, The Railroads of the South, 1865-1900:
    A Study in Finance and Control (Chapel Hill: University of North
    Carolina Press, 1965), p. 231.

165Overton, p. 201.

Chicago, Burlington and Quincy might adopt a simple device, such as
the familiar Western Union sign, which could be easily and quickly
comprehended and then "iterate and reiterate it constantly, that is to
say: place it in so many and so prominent places that the eye and
mind become familiar with it, and a mere glance is sufficient to
bring it before the mind that the fact of the road and its where-
abouts." Perkins also emphasized the importance of stability by
noting "Stability carries with it the idea of safety and regular-
ity."[166]

Touzalin agreed with Perkins' idea of a standard designation and
suggested that "the Burlington" rather than "the Quincy" be established as the name of the system and a logo be developed. Perkins con-
curred, and in 1885 the Chicago, Burlington and Quincy retained an advertising agency to place newspaper advertisements, order calendars
and fans.[167] Perkins' management team proposed to inform the country
about the services offered.

Apparently their marketing strategy was a success. S. F. Van Oss
in his 1893 book American Railroads as Investments, observed that the
Chicago, Burlington and Quincy "excels all others in advertising. By
constantly keeping its name before the public, this railway has made
its attractions known from the Pacific to the Atlantic." More specifically, Van Oss felt the Chicago, Burlington and Quincy's playing
cards on which the system's name was prominently displayed, "have

---

[166]Perkins to Potter, June 13, 1882, underlining in original, as
quoted in Overton, p. 202.

[167]Overton, p. 202.

become the principal implements of 'poker' between the lakes and the Gulf."[168]

IX. ANALYSIS, PLANNING AND DEVELOPMENT

	1870	1880	1890	1900
A T & S F	Average	Superior	Average	Average
B & M	Average	Average	Harmful	Average
C B & Q	Average	Average	Average	Average
I C	Average	Superior	Average	Average
L & N	Average	Average	Harmful	Average

Management's provision for the origination of ideas, processes, services, and procedures is appraised in this category. As noted in Category VIII, marketing effectiveness, the business enterprise has two basic functions: marketing and innovation.[169] Innovation calls for analysis, planning and development. Jenks defined those managers as innovators if they were "individuals who have so completely absorbed the role that they play it with a high degree of virtuosity and apparent autonomy." In essence, they are "creative."[170]

For example, in 1879, Perkins of the Chicago, Burlington and Quincy, warned against the needless forcing of the technological pace. He wrote to his general manager ten years later that "of one thing I am

[168]S. F. Van Oss, American Railroads as Investments (New York: Putnam's, 1883), p. 496-7.

[169]Drucker, Management, p. 61.

[170]Harvard University Research Center in Entrepreneurial History, Change and the Entrepreneur: Postulates and the Patterns for Entrepreneurial History (Cambridge, Mass.: Harvard University Press, 1949), p. 137.

very certain, that is that the character of the service is becoming more and more important, and we must keep up with the march of improvements in this respect, or we shall lose traffic."[171] Although one might expect that the competitive environments facing all five roads would give the road with the most innovation an advantage, Cochran's research cautions "there is no evidence" to support the gaining of "any longrun advantage or permanent leadership."[172]

There is some evidence that some managements recognized that certain existing arrangements were less effective or otherwise unsatisfactory and pressed for better solutions.[173] For example, Brooks suggested trying some homemade sleeping cars; Ackerman wanted the Atchison, Topeka and Santa Fe to make its own rails; Perkins worked out the details of a functional hierarchy of top executives of the Chicago, Burlington and Quincy and urged delegation and authority to improve the organization structure (see Category III); and, Fink of the Louisville and Nashville developed innovations in methods of finance (see Category III).

The period from 1870 to 1880 marked the introduction of a number of innovations in the railroad industry. The adoption of a standard track gauge; the increased use of steel rails; the introduction of

---

[171]Perkins to Forbes, 1879, as quoted in Cochran, p. 141.

[172]Cochran, p. 142.

[173]Ibid.

automatic couplers, better brakes, standard time;[174] more powerful locomotives; and better cars are all examples. Such innovations helped to lower rates.

The Illinois Central participated in most of these improvements and changes in rail technology. In fact, President Ackerman and General Manager Clarke even narrowed the gauge of their southern lines to the standard width five years before the rest of the South achieved this basic reform. Plans were begun in 1880 to eliminate the dual-gauge tracks and on Friday, July 29, 1881, the last spikes of the west rail were removed, and some spikes driven into place for the new gauge. As described by Stover,

> Starting at dawn...a section crew for each mile of track started to move the west rail inward 3½ inches. The work was carefully organized, with each crewman given a special task of pulling spikes, moving the rail, or driving spikes home to fasten the rail in the new position. The work was all finished by 3 p.m. that afternoon. When the other southern lines shifted to standard gauge five years later they followed closely the /same/ plans and procedures.[175]

When Milton Smith returned to the Louisville and Nashville, he evaluated the state of that road in terms that were anything but encouraging.[176] In noting that past managements had tried to

---

[174]As Stover, Illinois Central, p. 174 notes: "All lines in the country shifted to standard time in the fall of 1883. Before this reform a quilt pattern of various times based upon various sun times was in use. For example, when it was 12:00 noon in Chicago it was 12:09 in Louisville, 11:50 a.m. in St. Louis, and 11:27 in Omaha. A person going from Maine to San Francisco might have to change his watch as many as twenty times, depending upon the route taken."

[175]Stover, Illinois Central, p. 188.

[176]Klein, p. 187.

economize on improvement expenditures by buying iron rather than steel rails, he declared:

> There has been no time during the past six or eight years when the management was justified in placing a single iron rail in any of the Company's main lines. In my opinion, the action of the past management in doing this cannot be satisfactorily explained or defended.[177]

In summary, the improvements during Smith's regime came from the continual growth and development of the network. Nevertheless, a myriad of minor changes provided for a significant total change. Perhaps even more important was the promotion of innovation in the iron, lumber, and other industries, both by providing demand and by altering the structure of the market; and the needs of the railroad for capital led to new methods of financing economic growth.[178]

X.   HEALTH OF EARNINGS

	1870	1880	1890	1900
A T & S F	Average	Harmful	Harmful	Average
B & M	Average	Average	Average	Average
C B & Q	Average	Harmful	Average	Average
I C	Average	Average	Average	Superior
L & N	Average	Harmful	Harmful	Average

Management's quality in this category has been previously defined as its ability to sustain company earnings and growth over time, considering the environmental circumstances. Both absolute and relative

---

[177]Ibid.

[178]Cochran, p. 144.

measurements are useful in analysis. Appendix C is offered to illustrate the results of the organizational activity of the five railroads.

As one of the service industries, railroads derive the bulk of
their revenues from the transportation of goods and individuals, although from time to time most roads transported express and mail. The
following figures are presented as illustrations of possible financial
data relating to the health of earnings situation for the five railroads. The data may be derived utilizing Appendix C and its twenty-
four columns scheme: Figure 5:3, Freight and Passenger Revenues;
Figure 5:4, Operating Revenues and Operating Expenses; Figure 5:5,
Dividend Payments; Figure 5:6, Passenger and Freight Mileage; and
Figure 5:7, Average Annual Revenues. In addition, Figure 5:1, Operating Ratios and Figure 5:2, Transportation Ratios as depicted in
Category VII operating efficiency, also relate to and have impact
upon health of earnings. The reader may wish to review the various
figures to gain an appreciation of each road's financial relationship.

Two means for measuring the efficiency of passenger and freight
service -- the two most important sources of railroad revenue -- are
volume and mileage. One method uses the number of passenger-miles per
mile operated and the number of freight-miles per mile operated. The
passenger traffic density combined with the freight density expresses
the degree of utilization of capital equipment.[179] The higher the line
for each of the roads on Figure 5:6, the greater the degree of utilization of the roadbed and probably the greater the use of the rolling
stock.

---

[179]Darr, p. 247.

123

FIGURE 5:3

FREIGHT & PASSENGER REVENUES
OF FIVE SELECTED RAILROADS

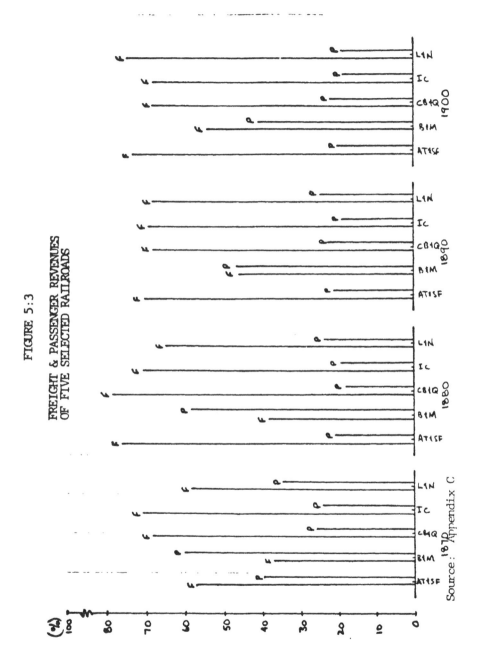

Source: Appendix C.

FIGURE 5:4

OPERATING REVENUES AND OPERATING EXPENSES
OF

FIVE SELECTED RAILROADS

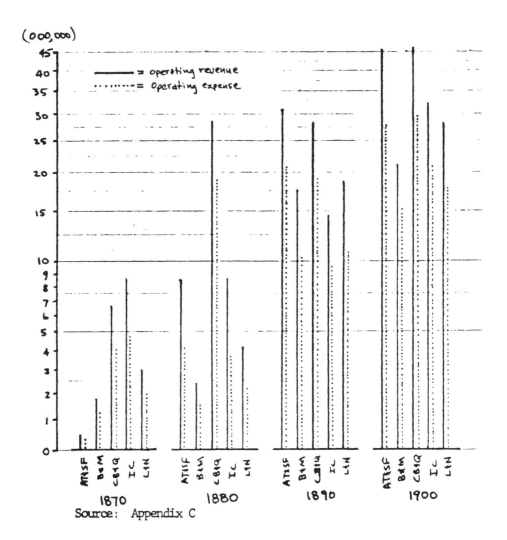

Source: Appendix C

FIGURE 5:5

DIVIDEND PAYMENTS
OF
FIVE SELECTED RAILROADS

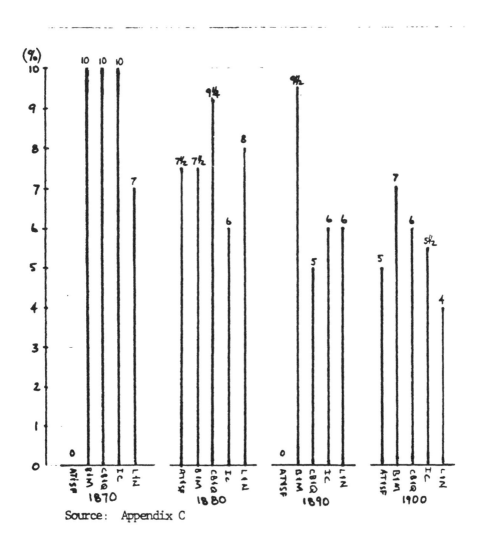

Source: Appendix C

FIGURE 5:6

NUMBER OF PASSENGER-MILES PER MILE OPERATED
AND TON-MILES PER MILE OPERATED
FOR
FIVE SELECTED RAILROADS

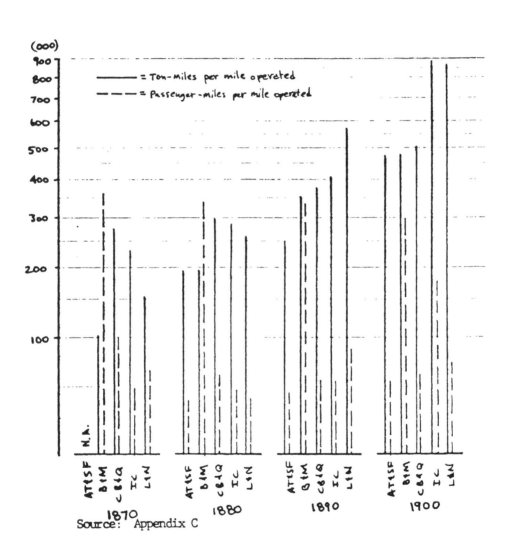

Source: Appendix C

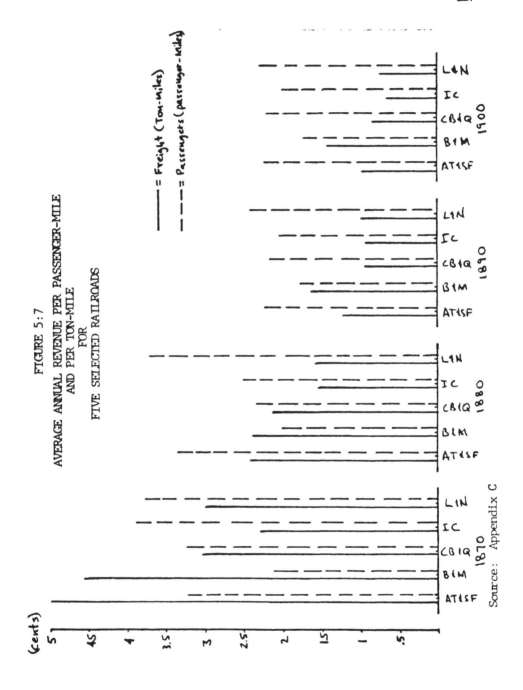

FIGURE 5:7

AVERAGE ANNUAL REVENUE PER PASSENGER-MILE
AND PER TON-MILE
FOR
FIVE SELECTED RAILROADS

——— = Freight (Ton-miles)

– – – = Passengers (passenger-miles)

Source: Appendix C

Average revenue per passenger-mile and average revenue per ton-mile indicates the possibility of profit with a given cost per passenger or ton-mile. Thus, with a given cost per passenger or ton per mile, the higher the line on Figure 5:7, the greater the profit per passenger per mile. The dividend records of the five roads, however, as noted in Figure 5:5 do not reflect such large fluctuations as Figure 5:7 might seem to indicate.

Operating revenue is the gross operating income from the passenger, freight and other services (see Figure 5:3), whereas operating expense is the total amount spent for the maintenance of roadway and motive power, transportation expense, salaries, insurance, etc. It is the cost incurred in moving passenger and freight traffic. Figure 5:4 relates operating revenues and operating expenses.

Comparisons between the five railroads encounter numerous difficulties. Each of the roads has distinct characteristics and thus comparisons should be viewed by recognizing differences such as (a) the geographical location, (b) the topography of terrain, (c) length of the road, (d) terminals, and (e) type of traffic predominating. Thus, comparisons should not be made without proper qualification. For example, the operating ratio (Figure 5:1), which shows the operating expense compared to operating revenue, may be of value for comparing an individual road's operating efficiency from one time period to another but not to compare two or more roads. On the other hand, one might compare the ratios of next income to operating revenue. (See Appendix C). Generally, the higher the ratio the more funds available for dividends and surplus. Darr declares, "It is this by which the owners

obviously measure the efficiency of their railroads and its managers."[180] A more common method for comparison was the dividend payments (Figure 5:5).

XI. SERVICE TO STOCKHOLDERS

	1870	1880	1890	1900
A T & S F	Average	Average	Harmful	Average
B & M	Average	Superior	Harmful	Average
C B & Q	Average	Average	Average	Average
IC	Average	Average	Average	Superior
L & N	Superior	Harmful	Average	Average

Appraisal of management in this category consists of safeguarding
the owners' (stockholders) capital from unnecessary risks or impairment, enhancing the principal, distributing profits as dividends at
reasonable and safe levels, and keeping the owners informed.

Illustrations as to health of earnings (Category IX) and dividend
payments (Figure 5:5) were previously illustrated as were ethics
(Category III). In general, it would appear that the small stockholder
was seldom aware of the leeway exercised in administrative control by
either management or boards. In fact, as Cochran notes,"it is impossible to equate strict sanctions on fiduciary responsibility in the
presidential role with good practice on the operating level...the
stockholder had, no doubt, many causes for complaint."[181] One area of

---

[180]Ibid., pp. 335-336.

[181]Cochran, p. 121.

concern dealt with the dissemination of useful information to the stockholders. Granted that annual reports were published, nevertheless, the timing and quality of many of them are limited. It is unlikely that a management would want to tell anything unfavorable unless it felt bound to do so because of common knowledge or curiosity. This matter of essential information for the stockholders, urged so strongly by early critics such as Henry V. Poor, was also stressed in the seventies by Brooks, Denison, and Forbes of the Chicago, Burlington and Quincy.[182]

Allocation of earnings to dividends was also another area of concern. Some men, such as Clarke, in writing about the 1888 Illinois Central dividend policy, said that an 8% dividend is an "absolute requirement."[183] Others, such as Smith of the Louisville and Nashville, believed that the system and its needs were paramount and that profits should be plowed back. This led the Louisville and Nashville board to relate that if Smith were allowed a free reign, the Louisville and Nashville might prosper and flourish but the stockholders would pay for the success with no income.

One of the most controversial questions regarding dividends was the issuance of stock dividends, or, as some critics referred to it, "watering the stock." Illustrations follow to show varying views.

Arguing for the practice, Forbes in 1869 thought that the Chicago,

---

[182]Ibid.

[183]Clarke, President (Illinois Central), to Jeffery, General Manager, 1886, as quoted in Cochran, p. 122.

Burlington and Quincy "policy has been well considered and successful:
if we had refused stock dividends we should either have refused in con-
sequence some of the connections and some of the improvements which
have proved so beneficial, and thus have escaped the dilemma of having
too much income to divide; or, if our income had kept up, we should
have had this year to divide 40 to 50% cash on our small capital."[184]

In contrast to what Forbes thought was right for the Chicago,
Burlington and Quincy, Osborn opposed stock dividends on the Illinois
Central when in 1869 he wrote,"there is so much bad work, watering railway shares by Vanderbilt and others, that we have decided to keep our
property very compact."[185] Later in 1880 he said, "In contrast to the
roads which are doubling their stock at this time, we are steadily per-
fecting our road. I don't believe in the policy of ...others watering
their stock whilst they have wooden bridges and trestleworks, and
station houses, and light rails."[186]

Once noted for the integrity and thoroughness of its reports as
pioneered by Albert Fink, by 1880 the Louisville and Nashville
accounting and reporting practices became the target of doubt and suspicion. Baldwin, president at that time, remained aloof to Wall Street
and stockholder questioning and commented that they were "almost all

---

[184]Forbes to Green, 1869 (Chicago, Burlington & Quincy), as quoted in
  Cochran, p. 121.

[185]Osborn to Peabody (Illinois Central), 1869,as quoted in Cochran,
  p. 122.

[186]Osborn to Ackerman (Illinois Central),1880, as quoted in Cochran, p.
  122. See also Appendix C for stock dividends and payment dates.

lies -- at least they are in the manner they are stated."[187] Such a
rejoinder did little to reassure Louisville and Nashville stockholders
of discrepencies in Annual Reports. As Klein notes in speaking of
this lowpoint in the Louisville and Nashville's history, "the asper-
sions cast upon the Louisville and Nashville grew worse as its reports
became progressively skimpier and more enigmatic. The lack of information, the dissension within management, and the widening credibility
gap on the company's exact financial condition all fed the rumor mills
and made credit difficult to obtain."[188]

Similar misgivings as to appropriateness of information were illustrated by the Atchison, Topeka and Santa Fe. During the reorganization
of the late 1880s various analysts criticized the road's statements.
Policy decisions, however, were of more concern to the stockholders.
For example, Railway Age raised some doubts about the Atchison, Topeka
and Santa Fe's fiscal position in 1887,but concluded that "the career
of this company has been one of the marvels of the railway enterprise,
and it would be unsafe now to attempt to fix a limit to its expansion
or the ambitions of its Napoleonic president and its bold and enterprising directors."[189] At the same time, the Commercial and Financial
Chronicle believed the same management to be too conservative in

---

[187]Commercial and Financial Chronicle , XXXIV (February 25, 1882), p.
216, as quoted in Klein, p. 196.

[188]Klein, p. 200.

[189]Railway Age, XII (1887), p. 325, as quoted in Stuart Daggett,
Railroad Reorganization (Cambridge, Mass.: Harvard University
Press, 1908), p. 198.

meeting competition.[190] Critics and proponents alike argued, and while there may be basic truths to be found in both sides, a financial crisis did develop which led to reorganization.

COMPOSITE OF CATEGORIES

This section depicts the composite ratings for the Atchison, Topeka and Santa Fe; the Boston and Maine; the Chicago, Burlington and Quincy; the Illinois Central; and the Louisville and Nashville Railroads for the years 1870, 1880, 1890 and 1900. The comparative management appraisals, Figure 5:8, is based upon a weighted average of each of the eleven categories (see Table 1, Chapter IV) and represents each railroad's management absolutely as well as in relation to the others.

It will be recalled that the separate categories were in no sense pure variables since each category dealt with several functions. As was pointed out in Chapter II, the function of an organization's management cannot actually be separated, so they tend to overlap and interlock in a total system. Thus, the composite reflects this weighting.

The point totals have been omitted and instead the road's management indicated as "Superior," "Average," or "Harmful" because the preliminary management audit point system of evaluation is not designed to provide statistical measurements and these appraisals of nineteenth century railroad managements are less complete than either Kennedy's Management Appraisal or management audits of today.

Figure 5:8 indicates several major changes in the relative

---

[190]Bryant, p. 150.

FIGURE 5:8

COMPARATIVE MANAGEMENT APPRAISALS OF FIVE SELECTED RAILROADS, 1870-1900

	1870	1880	1890	1900
SUPERIOR Definitely above average				A T & S F
AVERAGE Not dangerously weak in any category	B & M A T & S F C B & Q L & N I C	C B & Q B & M A T & S F I C	C B & Q I C	C B & Q I C B & M L & N
HARMFUL Certain functions were not performed effectively or were ignored		L & N	A T & S F L & N B & M	

position of each of the organizations for each of the four years as well as in relation to one another. For example, whereas the Boston and Maine's management was assessed superior in 1870 and 1880, it was appraised harmful in 1890 only to rise again in stature in 1900. This no doubt was in response to Tuttle's leadership. The Illinois Central's management appears to have hovered around the average mark indicating no overburdening areas of concern nor enough about average developments to push it into the superior category. The Chicago, Burlington and Quincy appears to be the most consistent in upper management comparative rankings; its management both absolutely as well as relatively was appraised superior or in the high range of average during the four different years studied.

It should be recalled that these appraisals are for every tenth year only, over forty years, and do not reflect continuity. For example, although the Atchison, Topeka and Santa Fe's management was rated harmful in 1890, in the 1887-1889 period it would have been assessed an even lower rating. Therefore, neither deterioration nor the improvement in management ability related to environmental circumstances, as shown in Figure 5:8. Obviously, if one were making a more complete management audit than is attempted in this manuscript, the explanation would constitute a continuous history of the company's management.

Findings, such as those noted above derived from the preliminary management audit, will be compared with Kennedy's more complete technique in the next chapter.

CHAPTER VI

COMPARISON WITH KENNEDY'S
MORE COMPLETE TECHNIQUE

The purpose of this chapter is to compare the preliminary
management audit with the Entrepreneurial and Management Appraisal
Technique (EMAT) as developed by Charles J. Kennedy. Since the
Boston & Maine Railroad is the only firm to which both techniques have
been applied, it will be used for purposes of demonstrating comparison.
To this end, (1) the findings from both techniques for the Boston &
Maine Railroad are compared, contrasted, and reviewed, (2) samples of
data available to each method are illustrated, (3) accounting and statistical variations are analyzed, (4) caveats are noted, and (5) the
usefulness of the preliminary management audit is discussed.

COMPARISON OF FINDINGS

The results and findings of the preliminary management audit for
the five selected railroads were elaborated in Chapter V. Figure 5:8
illustrates the overall appraisal of each road in terms of the general
categories of "Superior," "Average," or "Harmful." From his pains-
taking study of the Boston & Maine, Professor Kennedy has released to
selected scholars[1] his tentative appraisal of the fifteen major railroads

---

[1] Members of the five symposia on EMAT for Railroad Historians are:
I. A Symposium on Accounting. Held at Denver, Colorado,
   April 29, 1978.

which later formed the Boston and Maine Railroad System. His released data for 1840-1870 gives an appraisal for every tenth year with
data on the eleven categories combined into four groups. Also, he has
released his tentative appraisal of those roads for 1880, 1890, and
1900, but for these years he has announced only their rank under the
classifications A, B, and C, and as yet has not given any break-
down into categories.[2] It should be recognized that

Papers by L. E. Andrade, Illinois State University; Paul V.
Black, California State University-Long Beach; Jack Blicksilver,
Georgia State University; J. L. Bookholdt, University of Houston;
Allen L. Bures, University of Dubuque; R. Gary Dean, Creighton
University; Kenneth O. Elvick, Iowa State University; Charles
J. Kennedy, University of Nebraska-Lincoln; Robert H. Raymond,
University of Nebraska-Lincoln. With a comment by Richard
P. Brief, New York University.

II. A Symposium on Measuring Financial Strength and Operating
Efficiency of Early Railroads. Held at Los Angeles, April 28
1979. Papers by William Gary Baker, Washburn University of
Topeka; Paul V. Black, California State University-Long Beach;
Allen L. Bures, University of Dubuque; Frank L. Gile, University
of Evansville; Neal Higgins, University of Portland; Charles
J. Kennedy, University of Nebraska-Lincoln; Richard E. Olson,
University of Alabama; Philip R. Smith, Michigan State Univer-
sity.

III. A Symposium on Rates and Division of Rates by Early Railroads.
To be held in Billings, Montana, April 1980. Papers by Charles
J. Kennedy, University of Nebraska-Lincoln; Richard Darr,
University of Wisconsin-Riverfalls; James Doster, University
of Alabama; Frank L. Gile, University of Evansville; Richard
E. Olson, University of Alabama; K. Peter Harder, University
of Western Washington. With a comment by Jack Blicksilver,
Georgia State University.

IV. A Symposium on Measuring the Economic Function of Early Railroads.
To be held in 1981.

V. A Symposium on Kennedy's Use of Entrepreneurial and Managerial
Appraisal Techniques. To be held in 1982.

[2]Charles J. Kennedy, Chapters on the Boston & Maine Railroad System,
Vol. 2, Part 1 (Lincoln, Nebraska: College of Business Administration, University of Nebraska), p. 365.

Kennedy is presently rewriting his manuscripts and that we can expect from him the following two kinds of presentations. For the 1835-1870 period, he is writing a capsule history of each of the six largest and most important companies in his study. Each history will be a very succint narrative demonstrating his Entrepreneurial and Managerial Appraisal Technique in both descriptive phrases and tables for each of the eleven categories. It will be a continuous history not merely for every tenth year. For the period after 1870, when the fifteen major roads were rapidly leasing and merging each other as well as a large number of minor roads, he will weave into his original manuscript the continuous EMAT data he has compiled for the six most important roads. This presentation will be more detailed, being somewhat like the amount of detail found in the secondary works we have used for the roads compared in the preceding chapter.

Thus, to compare our findings with Kennedy's released findings, we have aligned them as follows: Superior = A, Average = B, and Harmful = C.

Bures	Kennedy 1870	Kennedy 1800, 1890, 1900
SUPERIOR management was definitely above average	85-100 Superior	A Better than Average
AVERAGE management was not dangerously weak in any category	70-84 Average	B Average
HARMFUL certain functions were not performed or were ignored by management	69 or less Harmful	C Poorer than Average

The overall findings of both Kennedy and this study (indicated as Bures'), are juxtaposed in Figure 6:1.

Several observations regarding Figure 6:1 are in order. First, although the rankings are not completely identical, overall the results are very similar. Discrepencies that exist (as well as similarities), are partly explained by the data or lack of data available to both Kennedy's study and this paper. This will be discussed further below. Second, although there may in fact be wider variations in the rankings done by Kennedy and Bures within any one of the eleven categories, the overall results are quite compatible.

Third, the overall evaluations done by Bures appear to be slightly "lower" than those done by Kennedy. This difference may in fact be due to the differences in data, Kennedy having at his disposal a great deal of data, while Bures worked with very limited resources. On the other hand, this difference might be explained by the analogy of two different instructors grading an identical essay without an adequate number of conferences to agree upon the same models for each grade category. Thus, without sufficient preliminary preparation, some evaluators will grade "higher," others "lower." For example, in Figure 5:8 it is seen that few of the mainline roads are judged superior in any of the years under investigation, although all five roads survived through tremendous struggles that threatened their very existence. For some evaluators, this capacity for survival might seem more significant. In any case, slight variations in the overall grading, as long as they are consistent, are more indicative of personal interpretations of the norm rather than

FIGURE 6:1

COMPARATIVE MANAGEMENT APPRAISALS OF

THE BOSTON & MAINE

	1870	1880	1890	1900
SUPERIOR Definitely Above Average	B&M (K)* B&M (B)	B&M (K) B&M (B)		B&M (K)
AVERAGE ... dangerously weak in any category				B&M (B)
HARMFUL Certain functions were not performed effectively or were ignored			B&M (K) B&M (B)	

B&M (K) = Kennedy's rating of the Boston & Maine

B&M (B) = Bures' rating of the Boston & Maine.

Source: Figure 5:8 and Kennedy, Volume 2, Part I, p. 365.

*Kennedy assigned 91 percent to the B & M for 1870, the highest of the fifteen roads he compared, although he states that figure may be revised downward and yet still be in the superior category when he completes his study.

anything else.

DATA AVAILABLE FOR EACH METHOD

It has already been pointed out in the preceding chapter that
one of the principle differences between a preliminary management
audit and Kennedy's entrepreneurial and management appraisal is the
quality and quantity of resources used for generating data. Having
an adequate data base is of supreme importance in both of these
methods. During the sixteenth conference on business history,
Marquis noted that "the limiting factor is the availability of
evidence."[3]

It has already been stated that the sources used for the preliminary management audit are mostly secondary. For the Boston and Maine,
the main sources were Poor's Manual of Railroads and three secondary
accounts. These accounts, although interesting and informative, are
definitely limited as compared to the mass of materials examined by
Kennedy. For example, Kirkland's excellent work Men, Cities, and
Transportation included ninety-five pages on the Boston & Maine;
Harlow's popular account for the years 1870-1900 has forty-eight
pages, and Bradlee's treatise includes eighty-four pages. Other minor
sources used for the preliminary management audit are even briefer.

On the other hand, Kennedy's voluminous sources included both
external sources and all of the inside records of the Boston and

---

[3]Lloyd K. Marquis, "A Comprehensive Framework for Analyzing the
Management of a Business Enterprise," in Papers of the Sixteenth
Business History Conference, ed. Charles J. Kennedy (Lincoln,
Nebraska: College of Business Administration, University of
Nebraska, 1969), p. 48.

Maine that are extant, such as the minutes of directors and stockholders meetings, miscellaneous reports and correspondence between
executives, testimony at certain hearings, analyses and news reports
from trade papers and newspaper, reports to the railway commission of
Massachusetts and to the I.C.C., and tariffs and other miscellaneous
sources. Clearly, the findings based on examining the secondary
accounts would seem tentative and inconclusive as compared to findings
from the material Kennedy examined.

VARIATIONS IN ACCOUNTING AND STATISTICAL DATA

In addition to the comparisons of narrative data, a discussion of
the variations between the accounting and statistical data found in
both methods is also in order. In general, the distinction between
accounting and statistical activities is not always clear, since both
deal with figures.[4] General accounting is a reckoning of receipts and
expenditures and a statement of balance in money terms. Accounts
indicate the financial results of operation and the financial condition of the enterprise. On the other hand, statistics are collected
and classified on a systematic basis to supply information regarding
the conduct of the enterprise, its efficiency and economy of operation, both in comparison with its own past record and with the record
of other and similar enterprises. In the railroads, these differences
were often obscured. Burnell points out:

---

[4]See for example, Association of American Railroads, Committee on Costs
and Statistics, Railway Statistics Manual, 3rd reprint (Washington:
Association of American Railroads, 1964), p. 101.

It is recognized that the numerous functions of railroad
accounting and statistics are so varied in character that
they cannot be reduced to an "exact" science, neither can
they be applied in like manner by all railroads. This
limitation depends to a great extent upon the human
equation and varying circumstances, such as differences in
organization, location and size of the railroad, and in
some cases to class of commodities handled.[5]

In this study, we leaned heavily upon the financial, accounting,

and statistical data either specifically stated or computed from Poor's

Manual of Railroads. This is in contrast to Kennedy's financial,

accounting, and statistical data derived from original sources and

stockholder, director, and state legislative reports. Selected

accounts and ratios for the Boston and Maine as compiled from Poor's

Manual and from Kennedy's manuscript are detailed in Appendix C. A

sample of these accounts and ratios are given in Table 6:2 for purposes

of comparison. Although only three columns are given in the table, any

of the twenty four columns included in Appendix C could be compared.

It will be observed that few of the values noted are identical.

There are several possible explanations which can be posed. First,

the classification of data may vary. For example, Kennedy's computa-

tion of property, Column 1, may include different items since he used

other asset accounts than did Poor. A second explanation may be a

difference in the year ending date. Also, a third explanation must be

posed which concerns not only the classification of data and the year

ending date but the accuracy of the data itself. The results of this

comparison with Kennedy's data cast doubts about the basis of Poor's

---

[5]Edward H. Burnell, Railroad Accounting and Statistics (Chicago:
Watson Publications, Inc., 1955), p. vi.

TABLE 6:2

SELECTED ACCOUNTS FOR THE BOSTON & MAINE

	Poor's Manual			Kennedy's Data		
	Property 1	Capital Stock (Paid-In) 2	Operating Revenues & Net Non-Oper. Income 6	Property 1	Capital Stock (Paid-In) 2	Operating Revenues & Net Non-Oper. Income 6
1870	$ 5,171,995	$ 4,471,275	$ 1,876,390	$ 5,474,253	$ 4,471,275	$ 1,876,391
1880	9,508,754	6,921,275	2,438,271	11,613,061	6,921,275	2,532,653
1890	27,876,355	16,297,744	15,531,191	32,254,048	16,297,744	14,587,026
1900	36,278,801	25,052,725	22,148,602	41,940,543	25,052,725	22,216,206

Source: Appendix C

accounting and statistical data. It must be remembered that Kennedy's data is based upon a lifetime's work of examining original sources as well as published governmental reports. Although Poor obtained his data from the companies themselves, apparently the data he received was not subjected to the same scrutiny that Kennedy exercised. If in fact Poor's published data is not totally dependable, then the conclusions drawn from that data cannot be completely accurate. This brings to focus one of the primary limitations of the preliminary management audit. If the sources used for generating data are inadequate or inaccurate, then a valid and precise preliminary management audit is impossible.

CAVEATS

There are several general caveats for those undertaking a preliminary management audit of a firm or organization. The first deals with the conclusions drawn. The preliminary management audit demonstrated in this study compared only four isolated years--1870, 1880, 1890 and 1900. No attempt was made to imply what occurred between these periods. For example, not shown in Figure 6:1 is the deterioration of the management under Frank Jones of the Boston and Maine during the middle eighties. The higher rating in the middle nineties was due in part to Tuttle's leadership. Consequently, the findings from this study should be viewed as representing only the four individual years examined and not necessarily the years in between.

The second caveat deals with the nature of the instrument itself. The management audit technique, whether it is used in a preliminary form or for a complete appraisal has inherent potential problems which should be examined. A potential problem area is the fact that the assigned quantitative values are based on subjective evaluations. Kennedy argues, however, that "a necessarily subjective rating scale carefully prepared and tested is better than a historian's judgment based only upon or heavily influenced by, intuition, inadequate evidence, or inadequately evaluated evidence.[6] In grading an essay examination, we know when we have read a superior, average, or poor paper judged both on its own merits (absolute) as well as in relation to others (relative). Scholars, also, after refinement in these techniques, could begin to agree on what is superior, average, or poor. However, the more we try to fine tune the scores, the greater is the possibility for disagreement. Just as college faculty may generally agree on "B" level work, they may not totally agree on B- or B+ work.

It would appear more useful to have a general measure (although approximate) of something we really want to know, than to bog down in disagreement on non-essential data.

Another concern regarding the management audit technique was expressed by Professor Blicksilver at the 1978 first annual Symposium on Accounting and Management Appraisal in Writing Railroad History. In his paper, Blicksilver expressed concern that 'Dr. Kennedy's

---

[6]Charles J. Kennedy, "Entrepreneurial and Managerial Appraisal In Writing Railroad History: A Suggestion for a New Approach to Business History," in Charles J. Kennedy, Comments on the History of Business and Capitalism, Especially in the United States. (Lincoln: College of Business Administration, University of Nebraska-Lincoln, 1979), p. 154.

disciples--as those of Frederick Jackson Turner--will lack the balance and disciplined scholarship of the master."[7] Such a concern has some validity. Moreover, researchers utilizing new research tools could fall into error if they are less than professional in their research. Conscientious scholarship always makes a significant difference in whether a research tool can be used effectively.

The third caveat, noted earlier in this chapter, deals with the need for necessary data. As stated previously, lack of data is perhaps the most limiting of all factors in conducting a management audit. Individuals are not available for questioning as would be available for a contemporary management audit. In addition, previously recorded data useful as evidence may be lacking or incomplete.

USEFULNESS OF THE PRELIMINARY MANAGEMENT AUDIT

The preliminary management audit compared with Kennedy's management appraisal technique appears to provide the following advantages:

(a) It provides a questionnaire checklist to organize research data. Such a checklist of things to look for when reading source materials and secondary accounts provides a useful technique to aid in the research and writing of business history.

---

[7]Jack Blicksilver, "Comments in Symposium on Accounting and Management Appraisal in Writing Railroad History," to be published by EBHA press 1980.

(b) It provides a guide to evaluate managements and the organization's strengths and weaknesses over time. Thus the preliminary management audit allows a basis for a tentative evaluation.

(c) It provides a basis of comparison between various organizations over various time periods in the same industry (the procedure utilized in this study), as well as the possibility of comparisons within other industries and hopefully between industries and eventually internationally. Such comparative analysis could be a powerful contribution to understanding.

(d) It provides a rating device to measure managerial competence, allowing for environment circumstances.[8] Although this study did not provide precise measurements, it did categorize managements as superior, average, or poor. Such research provides the beginning of the research necessary to provide models of various managerial competence. Once such models have been completed, additional comparative analysis would be possible.

(e) It provides a guide to allow the business historian to write more than a mere narrative. The preliminary management audit thus allows one to consider evidence more carefully.

---

[8]In Kennedy's words, his "hypothesis, tested in the field of New England railroad history, /is7 that not merely performance but ability, sharpened and developed in repeated, hard circumstances, has made superior performance possible whereby the businessman within the limit of the conditions affecting his work, created or changed institutions to meet his need." Stated in broadside announcing courses offered by Charles J. Kennedy for 1980-1981 (n.d.).

(f) It provides an approach, a paradigm, to meet the need for
another approach to our understanding of our economical
business history. The preliminary management audit and
Kennedy's technique offer an analytical approach.

What emerged from the comparison of the preliminary management
audit and Kennedy's full management appraisal, is the potential for
a new paradigm. Although Kennedy's approach is a more refined and
developed technique than the preliminary management audit utilized
in this study, both provide a valuable tool for the business historian.
Otherwise, as Kennedy notes, "we /must/ rely upon a quantification
interpretation of economic history which gives little attention to
the individual, or else we turn to institutional and narrative
histories." Together with the management audit techniques such
approaches would help us to more fully understand the development of
the American Business System.

CHAPTER VII

USEFULNESS OF A PRELIMINARY

MANAGEMENT AUDIT AND

CONCLUSIONS

This dissertation has dealt with the preliminary management audit as a technique to aid in the writing of business history. The purpose of this study has not been to make specific assertions about the relationship of successive managements to the overall performance of a firm or to the development of the economy, but rather to provide a methodological tool for measuring, analyzing, and comparing managements as an aid to the business historian. The preliminary management audit was posed as a workable, adequate, acceptable procedure for gathering and analyzing data, and comparing longitudinally the quality of management existing in various firms or organizations. The railroad industry was utilized for this purpose because (1) prior to 1870 it was the nation's only big business and (2) Kennedy has used management appraisals in his research of early railroads.

As a beginning contribution to the research needed, this study established criteria and examples of managerial expertise from a sample of the nation's first large-scale organization--the railroads. To accomplish this task the findings from a preliminary management audit for the years 1870, 1880, 1890, and 1900 for five selected railroads were discussed. The findings from one of the five selected railroads--

The Boston and Maine--were compared to findings from a more complete
management appraisal conducted by Kennedy. Finally, certain caveats
were given in the use of the preliminary management audit as a method
of writing business history. The results of the preliminary management audit conducted on the five selected railroads, are only tentative
in nature. It was found that in many cases there was insufficient useful data, and in some cases the completeness of the data available was
questioned. In spite of this, there was a high level of correspondence between the overall results of the preliminary management audit
and the complete management appraisal conducted by Kennedy with regard
to the Boston and Maine. However, caution appears warranted concerning the overzealous use of precise figures or qualification to
audit or appraise a firm's management when the evidence is quite
limited. This same caution was noted by the AIM concerning the
availability of evidence as being the limiting factor.

The conceptualization of the preliminary management audit as a
tool--a procedure for systematically examining, analyzing, and appraising a management--is one thing; the operationalization is another.
This study is a beginning contribution to the research necessary to
more fully operationalize the preliminary management audit.

A number of complex developmental issues must be resolved if the
preliminary management concept is to be more effectively operation-
alized as an aid in the writing of business history.

First, an operational taxonomy must be more fully developed that
effectively defines each of the categories. Revisions and/or alterations in the categories as established by Kennedy might be made for

industries other than railroads; however, the basic format would remain the same.

A second fundamental concern is to refine instruments and techniques for applying the categories to locatable data. Essentially this problem centers on (1) the development of standardized data, (2) the acquisition of that data, and (3) the development of data collection instruments to translate organizational, private, public and other research data into the appropriate categorical dimensions included in the Kennedy's appraisal guide.

A third major issue is the necessity of establishing a commonality of terms and language as well as agreement on what constitutes the ratings "excellent," "superior," "average," "harmful," "mediocre," etc. A paradigm of management excellence with illustrations from various organizations must be developed. For this purpose, future studies of other railroads, along the lines demonstrated in this study would be of great value in this endeavor, providing the individual authors would confer frequently in symposia or other meetings.

A fourth concern deals with the exploration of the possibility of comparing a given organization in one generation with the same organization in a subsequent generation to note what change has come about, if any, in the progress of its management. Related would be comparisons between managements of firms of one industry (e.g. railroads) and managements of firms in other industries (e.g. steel). Appropriate alterations in category and questionnaire design may therefore enable comparisons regarding management competence and the role of those managers both interfirm and interindustry over time.

A fifth concern is the development of a computer software system code capable of effectively and efficiently processing the data involved in operationizing the preliminary management audit. Developing this code would require consideration of such factors as input/output models, formats, storage requirements, data analysis options, advantages of various programming languages, system hardware compatibility and retrieval.

FUTURE DIRECTIONS

Full consideration of the preliminary management audit as a comprehensive and systematic appraisal tool will require additional discussion and dialogue. I would propose that additional dialogue in the form of additional doctoral dissertations and national symposia be promoted to deal with the following issues and their relationship to management appraisal techniques:

1- Environmental Setting. Any study, analysis and evaluation of an organization should include a study of the environment as well as a study of the anatomy of the organization. The "fit" as determined by management is after all an attempt to act and react to environmental forces. The importance of this was detailed in Chapter II of this paper.

2- Financial Analysis. Financial analysis is one of the more important tools for evaluating the health of an organization both as a whole and with its subdivisions. Figures are more precise than words and can be of enormous value to the researcher in determining relationships and discovering symptoms of basic problems. A common data base for financial analysis must be developed.

3- <u>Marketing.</u> In measuring a firm's marketing effectiveness, a researcher first of all needs to know whether the firm subscribes to the marketing concept of satisfying the wants and needs of the consumer at a profit. The importance of the marketing mix (product, place, promotion, and price) to the firm should be explored in greater detail.

4- <u>Engineering</u> and <u>Research</u> and <u>Development.</u> The role of engineering and research within the organization is to contribute to the profitability of the firm by providing technical support for the formulation and implementation of the organization's objectives. This, too, should be considered.

5- <u>Human</u> <u>Resources.</u> The researcher should not concentrate purely on technical solutions to general management and functional problems and issues. It is people who cause problems, correct problems, and prevent future problems. The staffing, training, and motivating procedures used in an organization are of utmost importance in the success of that organization.

6- <u>Management</u> <u>Audit</u> <u>Approach</u> <u>vs.</u> <u>Other</u> <u>Management</u> <u>Analyses.</u> This is a broader issue but most deserving of attention. Functional analysis, entrepreneurial analysis, and intuitive analysis could, for example, be compared with the management appraisal approach in general and the preliminary management audit in particular. Such dialogue could result in greater agreement on the content of each audit category. Appropriate

questionnaires could be designed and illustrations of various
levels of management competence developed.

The use of management audits in a more refined or preliminary
form as a comprehensive and systematic appraisal tool utilizing a
checklist approach to the evaluation of management functions and
company operations and decisions appears warranted.

Despite the significant practical problems to be resolved, this
approach to writing business history offers the theorist and researcher a real and potential framework for the evaluation of the role
of management and their organizations.

However, if the management audit approach to writing business
history is to realize its potential as an effective construct, its
development must proceed in a systematic, unified and directed manner.
Kennedy's Appraisal Guide for American Railroads is offered as an example of a conceptually pragmatic, research-based framework with considerable potential for use in writing railroad history. With adap-
tations it could be utilized to evaluate other organizations in other
industries as well.

In summary, the management audit approach adopted to writing
business history can be used to:

1- Provide a questionnaire checklist to organize research data.

2- Provide a basis of comparison between various firms or organizations over various time periods (given necessary category
and questionnaire alterations).

3- Provide a guide to evaluate managements and an organization's
strengths and weaknesses over time.

4- Provide a rating device to measure managerial competence. This requires research to build "models" of both excellent and average management competence. Once such models have been completed, the appraisal of managements of other firms in that industry can be made.

The significance of the foregoing is that we have set out to determine an evaluation technique which can be used by any researcher in economic and business history. The preliminary management audit along with a well-developed questionnaire and illustrations will hopefully contribute to a better understanding of management competence as a factor in the development of organizations and their subsequent impact upon economic, political and social progress.

APPENDICES

APPENDIX A

KENNEDY'S GUIDE TO THE ANALYSIS AND APPRAISAL OF THE

MANAGEMENT OF AMERICAN RAILROADS, 1830-1870*

I. (6%) ENTREPRENEURSHIP

    A. What did the railroad attempt and accomplish in interline
        freight traffic?
    B. What did the railroad perceive as an opportunity in carrying
        mail, parcels, and small lots of freight? What did it do
        about such opportunities?
    C. Did the managers "continually scrutinize (and revitalize)
        their plan to keep in touch with changing realities?"
        (See Lloyd K. Marquis, "A Comprehensive Framework for
        Analyzing the Management of a Business Enterprise," in
        Charles J. Kennedy (ed.), Papers of the Sixteenth Business
        History Conference, February 21-22, 1969, p. 42.

II. (6%) SOCIAL RESPONSIBILITY

    A. How and to what extent did the railroad contribute to the
        actual expansion of markets? (Consider (1) construction
        of sidings, (2) convenient schedules, (3) attractive
        rates.)
    B. Where, how, and to what extent did this railroad contribute
        a heretofore unmet need in passenger transportation, such
        as commuters, local, and interline? (Consider (1) new lines,
        (2) speed, (3) comfort, (4) dependability, (5) safety,
        (6) and low freight rates to facilitate the development of
        resort hotels.)

---

*Source: First presented as ten categories (I and II above labeled
as Economic Function) in Charles J. Kennedy, "Management Appraisal
for Historians," a handout to his Seminar in Economic and Business
History at the University of Nebraska-Lincoln, copyright 1971, later
published in Charles J. Kennedy, Comments on the History of Business
and Capitalism, Especially in the United States, (Lincoln, Nebraska:
College of Business Administration, University of Nebraska-Lincoln,
1974), pp. 161-165, reprinted in A New Approach to the History of the
American Business System, (Lincoln, Nebraska: College of Business
Administration, University of Nebraska-Lincoln, 1979), pp. 35-43. The
above version will appear in the author's Railroad History: Entrepreneurial and Managerial Appraisal and Other Essays.

C. Did the railroad cooperate with the communities, such as providing grade crossings, attractive depots and grounds, and desired schedules?

D. What did the railroad do for its employees besides merely employing them?

E. What was the railroad's reputation as a business concern, especially in its relation to the local community?

F. Did the railroad or its management participate in projects sponsored by other organizations in the community or by the town or city government?

III. (5%) ORGANIZATION STRUCTURE

A. What positions did the president hold?
(President of company; president of board; chairman of finance committee, etc.)

B. Was the board of directors large or small? How many members appeared to be quite active and knowledgeable?

C. List the committees of the board. What was the nature of their activities? How often did they meet?

D. Did the directors formulate any policy or merely approve what the president and one or two other men presented?

E. Did the railroad engage outside services, such as legal services, financing, stock transfer, production of engines and rolling stock?

F. Did the company use the inside contract system, such as handling freight at terminal freight depots?

G. Did one or a few stockholders dominate the management? What is the evidence?

H. Were there stockholders' protests? What was the occasion, the nature, and the result? Who was the leader of the protest?

I. Did the railroad own or control any other railroads, terminal properties, bridges, or vessels? Designate if stock ownership, guarantee of bonds, etc. Show the extent of control or influence.

J. List the titles and jurisdiction of the chief officials. Indicate the line of authority. Was there a clear distinction between responsibility and accountability? (See Marquis, p. 44.)

K. Was there any indication of concern about organizational change to improve the effectiveness of the company?

IV. (20%) EXECUTIVE ABILITY

A. What appeared to be the practice or plan for recruiting, training, compensating, and promoting officials?

B. Was the communication and teamwork between the officials themselves and between the officials and other employees of high or low quality? Indicate the evidence.

C. Was there a reasonable delegation of authority? Who was

accountable to the board of directors? Who was accountable
to the president, etc.?

D. Did the delegated authority match responsibility in
every respect?

E. Was there nepotism in the organization? What was the
effect?

F. How did the executives' salaries compare with similar
positions on other comparable railroads?

G. Did the full-time officials engage in any public activities? Specify.

H. Was there any evidence of provision for executive
succession?

I. How able was the president (or whoever was the top full-
time executive??

V. (8%) DIRECTORATE EFFECTIVENESS

A. Who were the members of the board and how long was each one
a director? Any evidence as to why each one was on the
board? Did they represent a wide range of background and
points of view?

B. Did the directors direct, or did they merely pass upon
proposals formulated by full-time officials?

C. List the committees of the board? How often did they
meet? Which ones were most influential?

D. Did the directors, through committees, engage in activities that could have been delegated to full-time officials?
Any evidence why this is so?

E. What was the attendance record of each director?

F. To what extent did the president or any other one or
two members dominate the board?

G. Any evidence that the directors truly acted as concerned
and responsible trustees for the stockholders?

H. Did the directors appear to actually select the chief
officials or did they merely give their assent to
recommendations by the president or other dominant
members?

VI. (10%) FISCAL POLICY

A. What was the ratio of debt to paid-in capital stock?
Was the debt largely funded or unfunded?

B. What was the provision or practice to finance the replacement of rolling stock (including locomotives),
track, and buildings? Did the method work? Did it
represent a compromise between short-run and long-run
financial benefits?

C. How was expansion financed and what changes occurred
in the capital structure?

D. How much attention was given to the equivalent of the
modern concepts of

(1) operating ratio
(2) times fixed charges earned, and
(3) the percentage available for dividends?
Indicate if the company was strong or weak in each of these categories.

E. Was fiscal policy the reason that the dividend rate and the market price of the stock were not higher? Indicate the evidence.

F. Was there any form of budgetary control or projecting of income and outgo?

G. Was there any evidence of financial reports for use by the top executives being more frequent than monthly?

H. What were the trends in revenue per ton-mile and revenue per passenger-mile? Did they reflect sound fiscal policy or were other factors partly responsible?

VII. (11%) OPERATING EFFICIENCY

A. How much attention was given to the modern concepts of
(1) the transportation ratio,
(2) average freight trainload,
(3) freight traffic density (ton-miles per mile operated),
(4) passenger traffic density (passenger miles per mile operated)?
Was the company strong or weak in those categories?

B. If there is sufficient evidence, determine if there was any growth in productivity per employee? Did the management appear to be interested in the concept of productivity?

C. Did the superintendent (or general manager if there was one) operate mainly in the yards or from behind an office desk?

D. Was there a significant difference in local load-factors by route segments, outbound and inbound?

E. What were the interline agreements? Were any unprofitable and what was done about it?

F. How were employee grievances handled? Any indications of labor disputes?

G. What indication was there of anything resembling modern job evaluation and merit rating?

H. How long and how many days a week did employees work?

I. What is the evidence of labor turnover?

VIII. (13%) MARKETING EFFECTIVENESS

A. How did the management determine the freight rates and the passenger rates, both local and interline?

B. What did the company do in advertising or "publicity"?

C. Was there any evidence of what has since been called market research and analysis?

D. What was the relation with express companies and milk contractors, if any? Were the contract prices remunerative to the railroad?

E. Was there any constructive policy to improve shipper and passenger relations?

F. Did the management appear to be aggressive in sales vigor or was there an attitude of merely serving the customer when he arrived or said he had a shipment?

IX.   (8%) ANALYSIS, PLANNING, AND DEVELOPMENT

A. Was the railroad responsible for any pioneering developments in passenger service and rates, such as
   (1) commuter services,
   (2) mileage tickets,
   (3) parlor car services,
   (4) sleeping car services,
   (5) excursion fares,
   (6) encouragement of residential suburbs, and
   (7) encouragement of resort hotels?

B. Was the railroad responsible for any pioneering developments in the movement of freight by
   (1) introducing incentive freight rates (specify what kind)
   (2) building or equipping special cars,
   (3) building or modifying locomotives,
   (4) making or experimenting with traffic control and safety devices, and
   (5) constructing sidings for customers?
   (What were the financial arrangements?)

C. What did the railroad do to improve the design, effectiveness, or lower cost of roadbeds, superstructure, and bridges?

D. Did the management or certain officials cooperate with any professional organizations or with informal groups of railroad officials in what has since been called research and development?

E. What evidence is there of trade books and periodicals read by the management, including the chief mechanic?

X.   (6%) HEALTH OF EARNINGS

A. Recasting the income statement according to the present I.C.C. requirements, what percent of the railway operating revenue was available for dividends? Consider the trend for ten or twenty years and compare with other railroads.

B. Using the same recasted income statement, how much was carried to the surplus or other unencumbered funds after the payment of dividends? (That is, were nearly all of the available funds used to pay dividends?) Consider the trend for ten or twenty years and compare with other railroads.

C. Do the earnings show only a relation to the growth of the

population and national income or did a part of the
earnings come from aspects of business new to this road?

D. During the years of depressed business conditions what
was the company's record of earnings? How did that
compare with other railroads? (If most railroads were
paying out nearly all of their earnings as dividends,
use the dividend rate for comparison.)

E. Approximately what percent of the railroad's business
came from low paying types of business? (Probably long-
haul freight and commuter passengers.)

F. Did the earnings show an increasing rate of return on
equity?

XI. (7%) SERVICE TO STOCKHOLDERS

A. What percentage of earnings available for dividends was
paid out as dividends?

B. How did this compare with other railroads?

C. Did the railroad ever withhold expenditures for (i) maintenance, (ii) renewal, or (iii) depreciation funds in
order to pay dividends? Did the railroad borrow to pay
dividends?

D. What was the practice of the management to enhance both
earnings and net worth? How did this compare with other
railroads?

E. What did the management do to maintain the company's
securities at specific price levels?

F. Were the annual reports to the stockholders sufficiently
informative and accurate so that the owners of the
securities could make rational decisions and participate
properly in the stockholders' meetings?

G. Were the dividends out of proportion to current additions
to "renewals" and earned surplus? Were the dividends so
high that in the future the railroad would be unable to
improve its roadbed and replace the ties and tracks and
the worn-out cars and locomotives?

APPENDIX B

ADJUSTING AND USING ACCOUNTING DATA*

CONDENSED BALANCE SHEET

(Figures in parentheses refer to columns in Appendix C, below.)

ASSETS

    1. Current Assets

(1) 2. Property (Total)

       2a. Operating

       2b. Non-operating

    3. Other Investments

    4. Other Assets and Deferred Charges

    5. Total Assets

LIABILITIES AND SHAREHOLDERS' EQUITY

    6. Current Liabilities

(3) 7. Long-term Debt

(4) 8. Other Liabilities (floating debt)

(2) 9. Capital Stock

---

*Source: Charles J. Kennedy, "Adjusting and Using Accounting Data As An Aid In Writing Railroad History, Especially 1830-1860," read at the Lexington Group of Railroad Historians, February 24, 1977, in Columbus, Ohio, later published in Charles J. Kennedy, Excerpts from Kennedy's Boston & Maine, (Lincoln, Nebraska: College of Business Administration, University of Nebraska-Lincoln, 1978), pp. 77-86. Will also be published in the author's Railroad History: Entrepreneurial and Managerial Appraisal and Other Essays.

9a. Common

9b. Preferred

(5) 10. Surplus

11. <u>Total Liabilities and Shareholders' Equity</u>

BALANCE SHEET RATIOS

12. Current Ratio (data in lines 1 and 6 in early years frequently unavailable or else requires an excessive amount of work)

13. Percent of Debt to Capital Stock

REVENUES

(6) 14. Operating Revenues (Total)

14a. Freight

14b. Passenger

14c. Express, Mail, Milk, etc.

(6) 15. Other income (If necessary, add "net" after the figure)

EXPENSES (deducted)

(7) 16. Operating Expenses (Total)

16a. Transportation Expenses

(8) 17. Taxes

(8) 18. Miscellaneous (including net hire of cars at a later date)

(8) 19. Fixed Charges

19a. Rents to other roads for entire facilities

19b. Interest for loans

20. Available Net Income

ALLOCATION OF AVAILABLE NET INCOME

21. Reserve Funds & Betterments (seldom used in early years)

(9) 22a. Common Stock Dividends

(9) 22b. Preferred Stock Dividends

(10) 23. Transferred to Profit and Loss (in early years, transferred to surplus)

INCOME ACCOUNTS RATIOS

(11) 24. Transportation Ratio

(12) 25. Operating Ratio

(13) 26. Times Fixed Charges Earned

(14) 27. Available Net Income as Percent of Gross Income

(15) 28a. Common Stock Dividend Rates

28b. Preferred Stock Dividend Rates

29. Return on Investment (very seldom used by the early
analysts)

OTHER STATISTICS

30. Common Stock Price Range (Par = 100)

(16) 30a. High for the year

30b. Low for the year

EFFICIENCY RATIOS

(17) 31. Revenue Tons per Freight Train

32. Net Ton-Miles per Freight-Train Hour (useless in early
Massachusetts when all freight trains commonly were re-
ported as moving at 10-15 miles per hour)

33. Net Ton-Miles per Car-Day (so far, we have been unable to
obtain "car-days")

34. Density of Traffic to Net Earnings (Compute by dividing the
sum of line 36 x 1/12 + line 35 with quotient of line 20 ÷
line 38 if the same as line 39. This assumes the average
passenger and his baggage weighed 1/12 of a ton.)

DENSITY

(18) 35. Ton-Miles per Mile Operated

(20) 36. Passenger-Miles per Mile Operated

     37. Passengers to and from Metropolitan Station (daily)

AVERAGE MILES OPERATED (average annual miles of line)

(22) 38. Freight

(22) 39. Passengers (Nearly always same as line 38 before into-
          duction of electric interurban lines)

PERCENT OF TOTAL REVENUE

(23) 40. Freight

(24) 41. Passengers

AVERAGE REVENUE

(19) 42. Per Ton-Mile (cents)

(21) 43. Per Passenger-Mile (cents)

APPENDIX C

SELECTED BALANCE SHEET ITEMS,

SELECTED INCOME ACCOUNT ITEMS,

INCOME ACCOUNT RATIOS,

AND

OTHER STATISTICS FOR:

APPENDIX C

The following outline of a condensed balance sheet and condensed income statement shows how certain items may be computed from the twenty four columns of statistics used in this appendix.

CONDENSED BALANCE SHEET	See Column	Compute from Columns
Assets:		
Operating property (road & equipment)	1	
Non-operating property		
Investments		
Current assets		
Total assets		
Stockholders' Equity and Liabilities		
Common stock	2	
Preferred stock		
Surplus, sinking, and contingent funds	5	
Funded debt	3	
Floating or unfunded debt	4	
Other current liabilities		
Total stockholders' equity & liabilities		

CONDENSED INCOME STATEMENT

	See Column	Compute from Columns
Railway operating revenues: Total	6	
Freight revenue		23 times 6
Passenger revenue		24 times 6
Other revenue		6 minus frt.& pass. rev.
Railway operating expenses	7	
Difference between revenues & expenses ("net revenue from railway operations")		6 minus 7
Taxes -------------------------------------		
Equipment & facility rents ---------------		
Net income from non-operating property and investments ---------------------	8	
Rent to other roads ---------------------		
Interest charges -----------------------		
Net income after fixed charges		14 times 6
Dividends	9	
Balance transferred to surplus	10	

TABLE C:1*

ATCHISON, TOPEKA, & SANTA FE RAILROAD

SELECTED BALANCE SHEET ITEMS

Year[a]	Property [b]	Capital Stock (Paid-in)[c]	Funded Debt	Unfunded (Floating) Debt	Accumulated Surplus
	1	2	3	4	5
1870	$ N.A.	$ 3,665,000	$ 2,765,000	$ -0-	$ -0-
1880	45,470,452	24,891,000	15,873,000	3,126,957	8,049,700
1890	330,849,780	102,000,000	231,655,470	5,833,300	770,134
1900	403,454,187	234,199,530	188,238,710	6,686,689	9,994,620

*Source: Tables C:1 through C:5 are derived from Poor's Manual of Railroads, 1871-72 through 1903, and J. G. Martin, A Century of Finance (Boston: J. G. Martin, 1890), pp. 150-154.

TABLE C:1 - continued

ATCHISON, TOPEKA, & SANTA FE RAILROAD

SELECTED INCOME ACCOUNT ITEMS

Year[a]	Operating Revenues & Net Non-Oper. Income [d]	Operating Expenses	Fixed Charges, Taxes, etc.	Dividend Payments [e]	Balance Carried to Surplus
	6	7	8	9	10
1870	$ 446,933	$ 295,304	$ N.A.	$ N.A.	$ N.A.
1880	8,556,976	4,101,158	N.A.	1,727,195	3,022,410
1890	31,004,357	20,920,386	N.A.	N.A.	770,134
1900	46,232,078	27,521,499	N.A.	3,139,556	4,414,491

TABLE C:1 - continued

ATCHISON, TOPEKA, & SANTA FE RAILROAD

| | INCOME ACCOUNT RATIOS | | | | | OTHER STATISTICS | | |
Year[a]	Trans-portation Ratio	Operat-ing Ratio	Times Fixed Charges Earned	Available for Dividends	Common Dividend Rate	Common Stock Price Range Par = $100 High	Low	Average Freight Trainload (Tons)
	11	12	13	14	15	16		17
1870	31.32	66.07	N.A.	N.A.	-0-	...	...	N.A.
1880	22.61	47.93	N.A.	55.51	7 1/2	113 3/4	152 1/2	103.02
1890	40.77	67.46	N.A.	N.A.	N.A.	23 3/4	50 5/8	138.98
1900	31.87	59.53	N.A.	16.34	5	N.A.	N.A.	239.46

TABLE C:1 - continued

ATCHISON, TOPEKA & SANTA FE RAILROAD

OTHER STATISTICS

Year[a]	Ton-Miles		Passenger-Miles		Average Mileage Operated	Percent of Total Revenues & Income	
	Per Mile Operated	Average Revenue (cents)	Per Mile Operated	Average Revenue (cents)		Freight	Passenger
	18	19	20	21	22	23	24
1870	N.A.	5.00	N.A.	3.22	509	57.32	39.28
1880	194,878	2.43	38,913	3.35	1371.91	75.96	20.88
1890	248,888	1.23	45,518	2.23	7110.95	70.10	21.32
1900	470,567	0.98	56,248	2.26	7341.34	72.96	20.19

NOTES FOR TABLE C:1

ATCHISON, TOPEKA, & SANTA FE RAILROAD

a. Each year is for a 12 month period ending on December 31, 1871 and 1880 and on June 30, 1890 and 1900.

b. Includes a small amount of non-operating property.

c. For the years 1871, 1880, and 1890 only common stock was used, however of the $234,199,530 noted for 1990, $102,000,000 was common and $114,199,530 was preferred stock.

d. The net non-operating income, a small amount, is included. However, column 6 is essentially railroad operating revenues and is used in computing columns 11, 12, 14, 23 and 24.

e. The dividend rates and dates were
    1870: -0-
    1880: February 2%; May 1 1/2%; July 2%; November 2%; total 7 1/2%.
    1890: N.A.
    1900: The dividend was on preferred stock only.

TABLE C:2

BOSTON AND MAINE RAILROAD

SELECTED BALANCE SHEET ITEMS

Year [a]	Property [b]	Capital Stock (Paid-in)[c]	Funded Debt	Unfunded (Floating) Debt	Accumu-lated Surplus
	1	2	3	4	5
1870	$ 5,171,995	$ 4,471,275	$ -0-	$ 450,000	$1,002,979
1880	9,508,754	6,921,275	3,500,000	89,777	1,761,995
1890	27,876,355	16,297,744	17,393,920	7,960,107	2,215,781
1900	36,278,801	25,052,725	21,330,334	9,687,239	1,519,753

TABLE C:2 - continued

BOSTON AND MAINE RAILROAD

SELECTED INCOME ACCOUNT ITEMS

Year [a]	Operating Revenues & Net Non-Oper. Income [d]	Operating Expenses	Fixed Charges, Taxes, etc.	Dividend Payments [e]	Balance Carried to Surplus
	6	7	8	9	10
1870	$ 1,876,390	$ 1,262,529	N.A.	$ 479,471	$ N.A.
1880	2,438,271	1,511,018	N.A.	525,000	163,525
1890	15,531,191	10,567,213	N.A.	1,042,211	14,084
1900	22,148,602	15,605,018	N.A.	1,515,304	22,016

TABLE C:2 - continued

BOSTON AND MAINE RAILROAD

	INCOME ACCOUNT RATIOS					OTHER STATISTICS		
	Trans-portation Ratio	Operat-ing Ratio	Times Fixed Charges Earned	Available for Dividends	Common Dividend Rate	Common Stock Price Range Par = $100 High / Low		Average Freight Trainload (Tons)
Year	11	12	13	14	15	16		17
1870	28.39	67.28	N.A.	N.A.	10	153	140	46.5
1880	30.21	61.97	N.A.	28.24	7 1/2	150 1/8	119	84.3
1890	22.54	68.04	N.A.	6.80	9 1/2	235	188	109.8
1900	26.99	70.46	N.A.	6.94	7	202 1/2	187	164.5

TABLE C:2 - continued

BOSTON AND MAINE RAILROAD

OTHER STATISTICS

Year[a]	Ton-Miles		Passenger-Miles		Average Mileage Operated	Percent of Total Revenues & Income	
	Per Mile Operated	Average Revenue (cents)	Per Mile Operated	Average Revenue (cents)		Freight	Passenger
	18	19	20	21	22	23	24
1870	103,190	4.58	361,592	2.14	146.13	36.78	60.16
1880	197,206	2.36	338,599	2.06	202.59	38.14	58.08
1890	357,221	1.65	337,590	1.80	1,210.03	45.84	47.31
1900	475,189	1.44	299,789	1.73	1,751.72	54.12	40.95

NOTES FOR TABLE C:2

BOSTON AND MAINE RAILROAD

a. The published returns by Poor's for 1870 covered only ten
months ending on September 30. However, Poor's added
two tenths to complete the year. Such adjustment affect
the other columns accordingly. The other years are for a
12 month period ending on September 30, 1880 and 1890 and
on June 30, 1900.

b. Includes a small amount of non-operating property.

c. The capital stock account includes $3,149,800 in preferred
for both the years 1890 and 1900.

d. The net non-operating income, a small amount, is included.
However, column 6 is essentially railroad operating
revenues and is used in computing columns 11, 12, 23 and 24.

e. Included in the dividend payments for 1890 was $94,491 for
preferred and for 1900, $188,988 for preferred.

f. The dividend rates and dates were:
    1870: January 5%; July 5%; total 10%.
    1880: November 4%; May 3 1/2%; total 7 1/2%.
    1890: May 4 1/2%; November 5%; total 9 1/2%. Preferred:
        September 3%; total 3%.
    1900: October 1 3/4%; January 1 3/4%; April 1 3/4%;
        July 1 3/4%; total 7%. Preferred: September 3%;
        March 3%; total 6%.

TABLE C:3

CHICAGO, BURLINGTON & QUINCY RAILROAD

SELECTED BALANCE SHEET ITEMS

Year [a]	Property [b]	Capital Stock (Paid-in) [c]	Funded Debt	Unfunded (Floating) Debt	Accumu-lated Surplus
	1	2	3	4	5
1870	$ 20,675,562	$16,590,210	$ 4,649,750	$ 2,157,723	$ 896,663
1880	109,641,187	54,413,196	44,093,925	16,453,010	119,419
1890	215,637,784	76,392,600	106,739,202	42,312,000	11,248,431
1900	233,602,755	98,447,500	134,174,100	39,418,000	15,722,392

TABLE C:3 – continued

CHICAGO, BURLINGTON, & QUINCY RAILROAD

| | SELECTED INCOME ACCOUNT ITEMS | | | | |
Year[a]	Operating Revenues & Net Non-Oper. Income[d]	Operating Expenses	Fixed Charges, Taxes, etc.	Dividend Payments[e]	Balance Carried to Surplus
	6	7	8	9	10
1870	$ 6,621,773	$ 4,003,882	$ N.A.	$ 1,520,790	$ 396,411
1880	20,454,495	9,362,904	N.A.	10,584,603	(4,296,849)
1890	27,725,967	18,749,699	N.A.	3,819,630	(302,435)
1900	47,535,420	29,816,838	N.A.	5,829,678	2,099,084

TABLE C:3 - continued

CHICAGO, BURLINGTON, & QUINCY RAILROAD

| | INCOME ACCOUNT RATIOS | | | | | OTHER STATISTICS | | |
| | Trans-portation Ratio | Operat-ing Ratio | Times Fixed Charges Earned | Available for Dividends | Common Dividend Rate f | Common Stock Price Range Par = $100 High | Low | Average Freight Trainload (Tons) |
Year[a]	11	12	13	14	15	16		17
1870	56.70	60.47	N.A.	28.95	10	162	145 1/2	N.A.
1880	25.43	45.77	N.A.	30.74	9 1/4	182 1/2	113 1/4	N.A.
1890	44.73	67.63	N.A.	12.69	5	111 1/2	81	N.A.
1900	31.54	62.73	N.A.	16.68	6	N.A.	N.A.	N.A.

TABLE C:3 - continued

CHICAGO, BURLINGTON, & QUINCY RAILROAD

OTHER STATISTICS

Year	Ton-Miles		Passenger-Miles		Average Mileage Operated	Percent of Total Revenues & Income	
	Per Mile Operated	Average Revenue (cents)	Per Mile Operated	Average Revenue (cents)		Freight	Passenger
	18	19	20	21	22	23	24
1870	276,954	3.06	98,742	3.26	532.25	68.18	25.94
1880	298,685	2.14	59,737	2.35	2,511.74	78.49	17.62
1890	383,474	.95	56,688	2.18	5,160.44	67.96	22.97
1900	502,666	.86	62,188	2.21	7,545.78	68.49	21.85

NOTES FOR TABLE C:3

CHICAGO, BURLINGTON, & QUINCY RAILROAD

a. Each year is for a 12 month period ending on April 30, 1870;
    December 31, 1880, and June 30, 1900.

b. Includes a small amount of non-operating property.

c. Only common stock was used. Capital stock outstanding on
    June 30, 1900 consisted of $98,446,100 of Chicago, Burlington,
    & Quincy stock and $1,400 of Boston & Maine Railroad (Iowa)
    stock. The authorized capital stock was $100,000,000.

d. The net non-operating income, a small amount, is included.
    However, column 6 is essentially railroad operating revenues
    and is used in computing columns 11, 12, 14, 23 and 24.

e. The dividend payment for 1870, 1890, and 1900 was in cash.
    The dividend payment in 1880 was $4,366,064 in cash and
    $6,218,539 in stock.

f. The dividend rates and dates were:
    1870: February 5%; August 5%; total 10%.
    1880: March 2%; May 1 1/4%; June 2%; September 2%; December 2%;
           total 9 1/4%. In addition a 20% stock dividend was
           granted in May.
    1890: March 1 1/4%; June 1 1/4%; September 1 1/4%;
           December 1 1/4%; total 5%.
    1900: September 1 1/2%; December 1 1/2%; March 1 1/2%;
           June 1 1/2%; total 6%.

TABLE C:4

ILLINOIS CENTRAL RAILROAD

SELECTED BALANCE SHEET ITEMS

Year[a]	Property[b]	Capital Stock (Paid-in)[c]	Funded Debt	Unfunded (Floating) Debt	Accumulated Surplus
	1	2	3	4	5
1870	$ 33,199,574	$25,278,710	$ 8,000,000	$11,050,932	$ -0-
1880	35,840,854	29,000,000	10,200,000	2,071,356	5,395,089
1890	89,888,699	40,000,000	62,662,000	2,962,870	4,493,966
1900	147,295,185	60,000,000	130,873,925	4,761,161	2,910,960

TABLE C:4 - continued

ILLINOIS CENTRAL RAILROAD

SELECTED INCOME ACCOUNT ITEMS

Year [a]	Operating Revenues & Net Non-Oper. Income [d]	Operating Expenses	Fixed Charges, Taxes, etc.	Dividends Payments	Balance Carried to Surplus
	6	7	8	9	10
1870	$ 8,678,958	$ 4,759,008	$ N.A.	$2,594,392	$ -0-
1880	8,304,812	3,672,971	N.A.	1,740,000	2,817,720
1890	14,448,006	9,565,104	N.A.	2,400,000	8,811
1900	32,611,967	21,377,615	N.A.	3,300,000	50,000

TABLE C:4 - continued

ILLINOIS CENTRAL RAILROAD

| | INCOME ACCOUNT RATIOS | | | | | OTHER STATISTICS | | |
| | Trans-portation Ratio | Operat-ing Ratio | Times Fixed Charges Earned | Available for Dividends | Common Dividend Rate | Common Stock Price Range Par = $100 | | Average Freight Trainload (Tons) |
Year	11	12	13	14	15	High 16	Low	17
1870	26.50	54.83	N.A.	29.89	10	N.A.	N.A.	163.4
1880	19.13	44.22	N.A.	54.88	6	N.A.	N.A.	110.2
1890	31.14	66.20	N.A.	16.67	6	N.A.	N.A.	130.7
1900	35.00	65.56	N.A.	10.27	5 1/2	N.A.	N.A.	221.7

TABLE C:4 - continued

ILLINOIS CENTRAL RAILROAD

OTHER STATISTICS

Year [a]	Ton-Miles		Per Mile Operated	Passenger-Miles		Percent of Total Revenues & Income	
	Per Mile Operated	Average Revenue (cents)		Average Revenue (cents)	Average Mileage Operated	Freight	Passenger
	18	19	20	21	22	23	24
1870	239,106	2.31	48,941	3.90	1,109.60	70.77	29.40
1880	288,855	1.54	47,947	2.51	1,320.35	70.84	19.16
1890	413,638	0.95	55,011	2.08	2,875.18	69.25	19.09
1900	890,874	0.65	79,482	2.02	3,845.43	68.32	18.94

NOTES FOR TABLE C:4

ILLINOIS CENTRAL RAILROAD

a. Each year is for a 12 month period ending on December 31,
   1870 and 1880 and on June 30, 1890 and 1900.

b. Includes a small amount of non-operating property.

c. Only common stock was used.

d. The net non-operating income, a small amount, is included.
   However, column b is essentially railroad operating
   revenues and is used in computing columns 11, 12, 14, 23
   and 24.

e. The dividend rates and dates were:
   1870: 2 payments of 5% each; total 10%.
   1880: 2 payments of 3% each; total 6%.
   1890: March 3%; September 3%; total 6%.
   1900: March 2 1/2%; September 3%; total 5 1/2%.

TABLE C:5

LOUISVILLE AND NASHVILLE RAILROAD

SELECTED BALANCE SHEET ITEMS

Year [a]	Property[b]	Capital Stock (Paid-in)[c]	Funded Debt	Unfunded (Floating) Debt	Accumu- lated Surplus
	1	2	3	4	5
1870	$ 13,950,705	$ 8,680,913	$ 8,478,000	$ 805,465	$ 748,977
1880	32,703,932	9,059,361	30,978,020	3,350,390	3,909,759
1890	77,790,155	46,989,020	57,643,910	5,142,310	-0-
1900	114,025,864	55,000,000	113,264,660	6,792,943	3,935,913

TABLE C:5 - continued

LOUISVILLE AND NASHVILLE RAILROAD

SELECTED INCOME ACCOUNT ITEMS

Year [a]	Operating Revenues & Net Non-Oper. Income [d]	Operating Expenses	Fixed Charges, Taxes, etc.	Dividend Payments [e]	Balance Carried to Surplus
	6	7	8	9	10
1870	$ 2,954,659	$ 1,812,525	N.A.	$ 607,696	$1,119,491
1880	4,377,418	2,279,942	N.A.	724,744	417,155
1890	18,846,004	11,419,092	N.A.	2,405,367	587,075
1900	27,742,379	18,603,406	$6,567,750	2,112,000	1,507,235

TABLE C:5 - continued

LOUISVILLE AND NASHVILLE RAILROAD

Year a	INCOME ACCOUNT RATIOS				OTHER STATISTICS			
	Trans-portation Ratio	Operat-ing Ratio	Times Fixed Charges Earned	Available for Dividends	Common Dividend Rate f	Common Stock Price Range Par = $100 High	Low	Average Freight Trainload (Tons)
	11	12	13	14	15	16		17
1870	N.A.	61.3	N.A.	58.46	7			N.A.
1880	20.33	52.08	N.A.	26.09	8			117.5
1890	26 53	60.59	N.A.	15.88	6			159.9
1900	35.43	67.06	N.A.	13.05	4			223.7

TABLE C:5 - continued

LOUISVILLE AND NASHVILLE RAILROAD

OTHER STATISTICS

Year[a]	Ton-Miles		Passenger-Miles		Average Mileage Operated	Percent of Total Revenues & Income	
	Per Mile Operated	Average Revenue (cents	Per Mile Operated	Average Revenue (cents)		Freight	Passenger
	18	19	20	21	22	23	24
1890	151,692	2.98	71,620	3.78	381.6	58.34	35.01
1880	255,252	1.61	38,636	3.72	1252.45	65.40	23.72
1890	569,079	0.98	87,206	2.42	2198.25	68.16	24.96
1900	858,543	0.76	73,895	2.31	3007.35	74.61	18.89

NOTES FOR TABLE C:5

LOUISVILLE AND NASHVILLE RAILROAD

a. Each year is for a 12 month period ending on June 30.

b. Includes a small amount of non-operating property.

c. Only common stock was used. The charter authorized the company
    to increase its share capital to an amount sufficient to
    represent in stock the full cost of the road and branches. The
    share capital as at present outstanding may be increased to
    $60,000,000 (by authority granted November 8, 1893) without
    further authority from the stockholders.

d. The net non-operating income, a small amount, is included,
    however, column 6 is essentially the railroad operating
    revenues and is used in computing columns 11, 12, 14, 23
    and 24.

e. The dividend payment was 4.9% in stock (3% in January of 1890,
    1.9% in July of 1890) and 1.1% in cash. The dividend payment
    for 1870, 1880, and 1900 was in cash.

f. The dividend rates and dates were:
    1870: February 3%; August 4%; total 7%.
    1880: February 3%; August 5%; total 8%.
    1890: January 3%; July 3%; total 6%.
    1900: February 2%; August 2%; total 4%.

TABLE C:6

BOSTON AND MAINE RAILROAD

(Kennedy's Data)

SELECTED BALANCE SHEET ITEMS

Year	Property	Capital Stock (Paid-in)	Funded Debt	Unfunded (Floating) Debt	Accumu-lated Surplus
	1	2	3	4	5
1870	$ 5,474,253	$ 4,471,275	-0-	$ 450,000	$1,002,979
1880	11,613,061	6,921,275	$3,500,000	134,263	1,861,995
1890	32,254,048	16,297,744	17,988,720	3,005,000	3,238,272
1900	41,940,543	25,052,725	21,925,134	-0-	5,365,885

Source: Charles J. Kennedy, Excerpts from Kennedy's Boston & Maine (Lincoln, Nebraska: College of Business Administration, University of Nebraska-Lincoln, 1978), pp. 103-112.

TABLE C:6 - continued

BOSTON AND MAINE RAILROAD

(Kennedy's Data)

SELECTED INCOME ACCOUNT ITEMS

Year	Operating Revenues & Net Non-Oper. Income	Operating Expenses	Fixed Charges, Taxes, etc.	Dividend Payments	Balance Carried to Surplus
	6	7	8	9	10
1870	$ 1,876,391	$ 1,237,859	$ 137,252	$ 455,000	$ 46,280
1880	2,532,653	1,404,766	439,885	455,000	233,002
1890	14,587,026	9,110,163	4,653,388	665,000	501,616
1900	22,216,206	15,135,114	5,851,780	1,325,899	236,734

TABLE C:6 - continued

BOSTON AND MAINE RAILROAD

	INCOME ACCOUNT RATIOS					OTHER STATISTICS		
	Trans-portation Ratio	Operat-ing Ratio	Times Fixed Charges Earned	Available for Dividends	Common Dividend Rate	Common Stock Price Range Par = $100		Average Freight Trainload (Tons)
Year						High	Low	
	11	12	13	14	15	16		17
1870	28.39	65.16	16.21	28.10	10	153	140	49.6
1880	29.58	55.47	3.06	27.17	6 1/2	150 1/8	119	84.3
1890	34.21	62.45	1.30	8.00	9 1/2f	235	188	106.7
1900	40.28	68.13	1.41	7.89	7	202 1/2	187	164.5

TABLE C:6 - continued

BOSTON AND MAINE RAILROAD

(Kennedy's Data)

OTHER STATISTICS

Year	Ton-Miles		Passenger-Miles		Average Mileage Operated	Percent of Total Revenues & Income	
	Per Mile Operated	Average Revenue (cents)	Per Mile Operated	Average Revenue (cents)		Freight	Passenger
	18	19	20	21	22	23	24
1870	91,090	4.29	299,340	2.14	174.13	36.26	59.30
1880	199,262	2.33	342,129	2.06	200,46	36.72	55.92
1890	328,483	1.71	325,988	1.81	1210.03	46.49	48.87
1900	470,130	1.44	293,863	1.73	1787.04	53.93	40.82

Source: Charles J. Kennedy, Excerpts from Kennedy's Boston & Maine, University of Nebraska: Lincoln, 1978, pp. 104-112 and Charles J. Kennedy's Manuscript Notes.

NOTES FOR TABLE C:6

BOSTON AND MAINE RAILROAD

a. Each year is for a 12 month period and ends as follows:
    December 31 until 1841 inclusive; November 30 for 1842-69;
    September 30 for 1870-85. Most data is based upon returns
    to the Massachusetts Legislature except the year 1870 which
    is based upon the Report to the Stockholders.

b. Column 1. Includes a small amount of non-operating property.
    See Table 16.

c. Columns 2, 9, 15. Only common stock was used. All of the
    stock was paid in cash. The total payments, including premiums,
    are included.

d. Columns 5 and 10: "Accumulated Surplus" includes both un-
    appropriated and appropriated earned surplus. Renewal funds,
    sinking funds, and surplus statements (called Profit and
    Loss) were included in the surplus by the Boston and Maine
    and other railroads. Column 5 does not necessarily reflect
    the exact amount carried from column 10.

e. Column 6. Is essentially the railroad operating revenues. The
    net non-operating income, a small amount, is included, but
    where the amount has been determined it is shown in table 16.
    The transportation ratio (column 11), the operating ratio
    (column 12), the percent of gross income available for
    dividends, (column 14), and the freight and passenger
    revenues as percents of the total revenues (columns 23 and 24)
    are computed by using column 6 as the division.

APPENDIX D

MAPS OF SELECTED RAILROADS

APPENDIX D:1

ATCHISON, TOPEKA & SANTA FE 1870

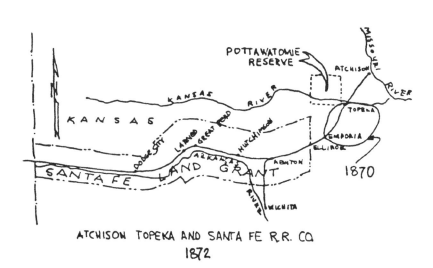

ATCHISON TOPEKA AND SANTA FE R.R. CO
1872

Based on Bryant, Atchison, Topeka & Santa Fe, p. 22 and Butterbaugh,
Atlas of Traffic Maps, pp. 118-119.

202

APPENDIX D:1 (continued)

ATCHISON, TOPEKA & SANTA FE 1880

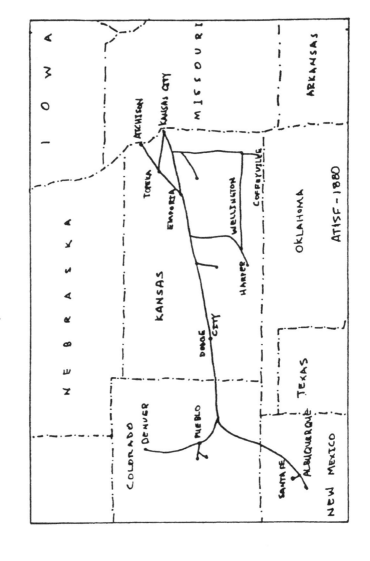

Based on Butterbaugh, Atlas of Traffic Maps, pp. 118-119 and Marshall,
Santa Fe, pp. 396-400.

203

APPENDIX D:1 (continued)   ATCHISON, TOPEKA & SANTA FE 1900

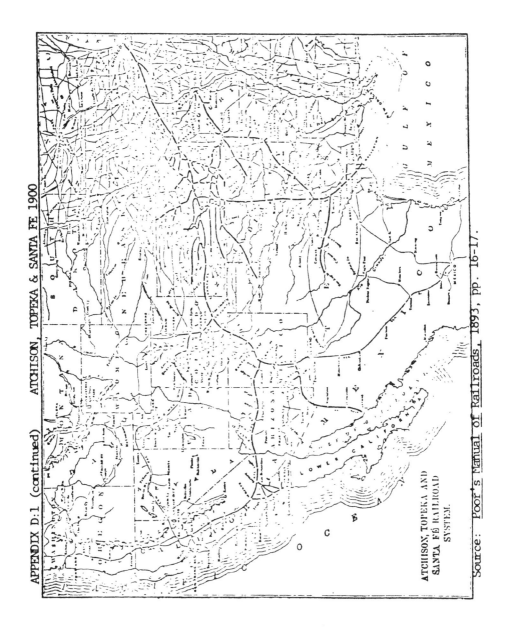

ATCHISON, TOPEKA AND
SANTA FÉ RAILROAD
SYSTEM.

Source: Poor's Manual of Railroads, 1893, pp. 16-17.

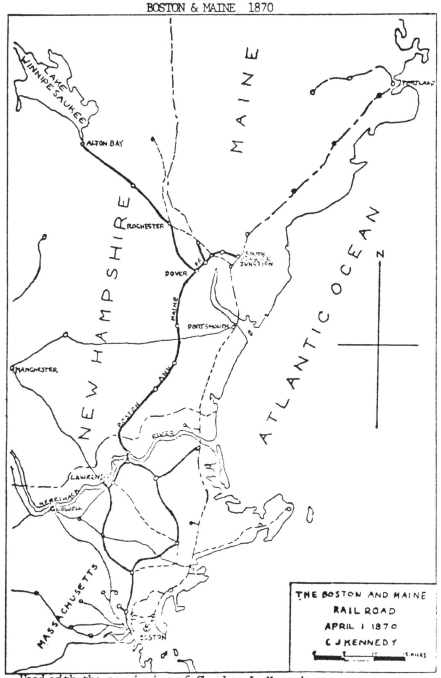

Used with the permission of Charles J. Kennedy.

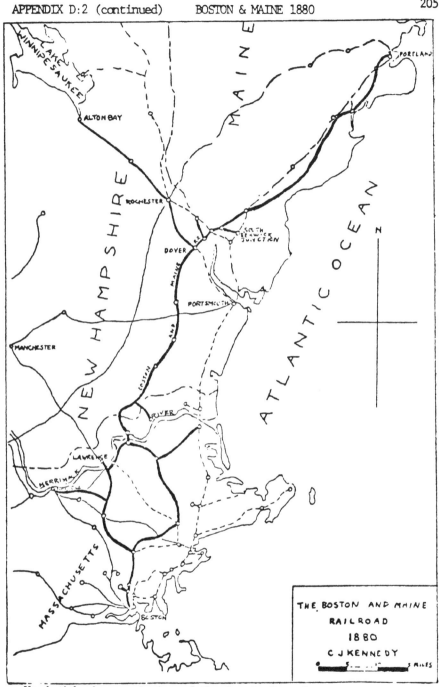

THE BOSTON AND MAINE
RAILROAD
1880
C J KENNEDY

Used with the permission of Charles J. Kennedy.

APPENDIX D:2 (continued)

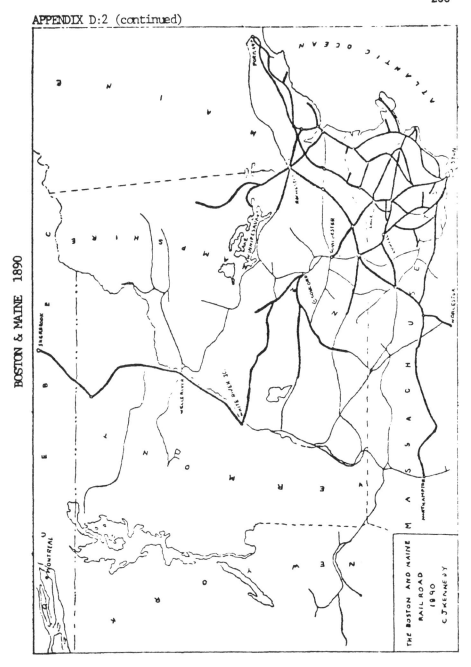

Used with the permission of Charles J. Kennedy.

APPENDIX D:2 (continued)

BOSTON & MAINE 1900

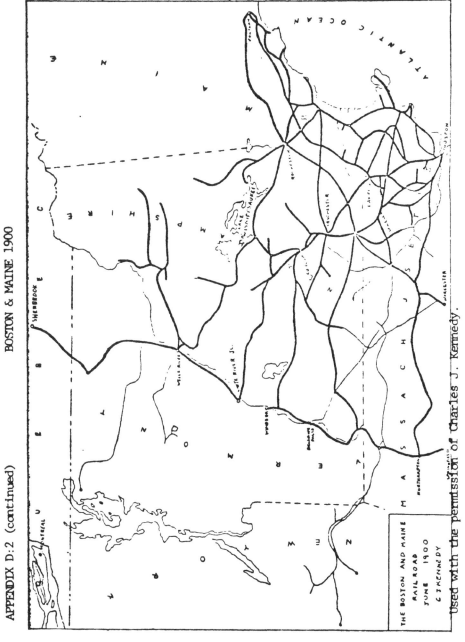

THE BOSTON AND MAINE
RAILROAD
JUNE 1900
C J KENNEDY

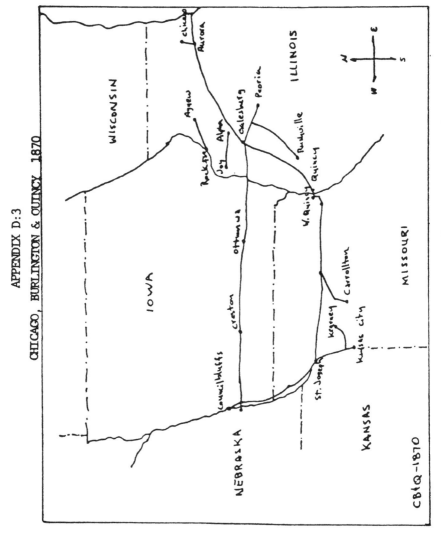

APPENDIX D:3

CHICAGO, BURLINGTON & QUINCY 1870

Based on Overton, Burlington Route, pp. 520-521 and Butterbaugh, Atlas of Traffic Maps, p. 130.

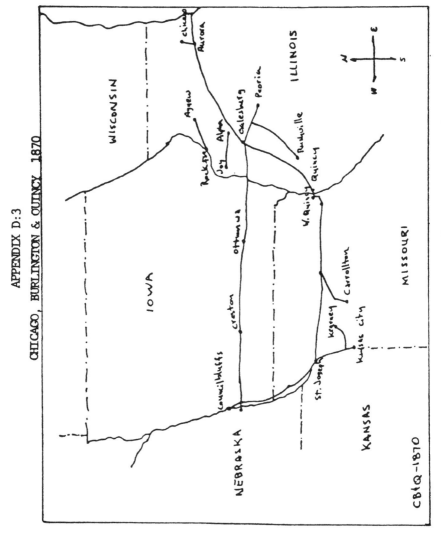

APPENDIX D:3 (continued)

CHICAGO, BURLINGTON & QUINCY 1880

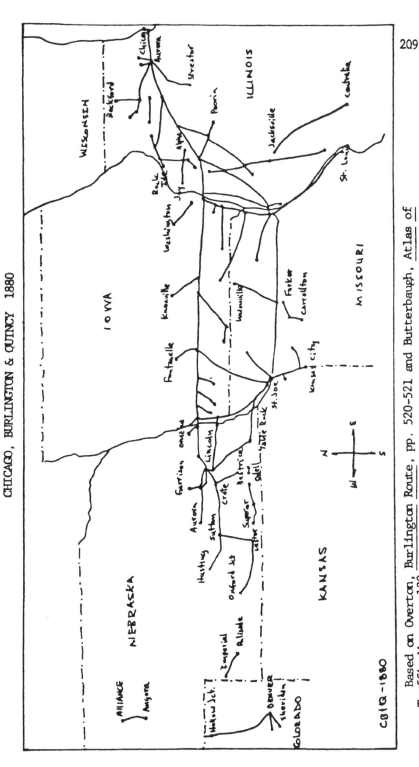

Based on Overton, Burlington Route, pp. 520-521 and Butterbaugh, Atlas of
Traffic Maps, p. 130.

209

APPENDIX D:3 (continued)
CHICAGO, BURLINGTON & QUINCY 1890

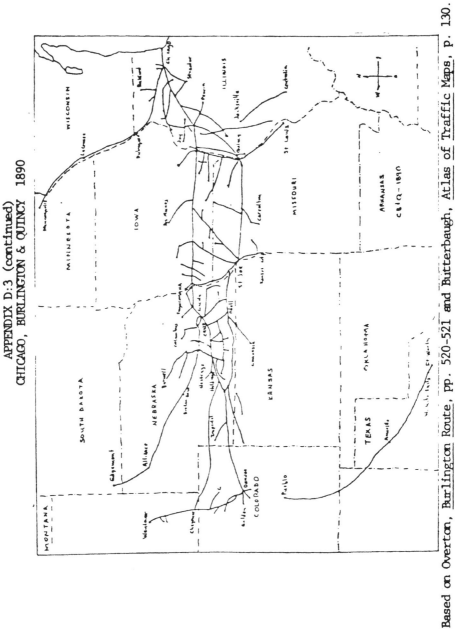

Based on Overton, Burlington Route, pp. 520-521 and Butterbaugh, Atlas of Traffic Maps, p. 130.

APPENDIX D:3 (continued)

CHICAGO, BURLINGTON & QUINCY 1900

CHICAGO, BURLINGTON
AND QUINCY R. R.
AND CONNECTING LINES.

Source: Poor's _Manual of Railroads_, 1900, p. 215.

APPENDIX D:4

ILLINOIS CENTRAL 1870

Based on Stover, Illinois Central, p. 134 and Butterbaugh, Atlas of Traffic Maps, p. 145.

APPENDIX D:4 (continued)

ILLINOIS CENTRAL 1880

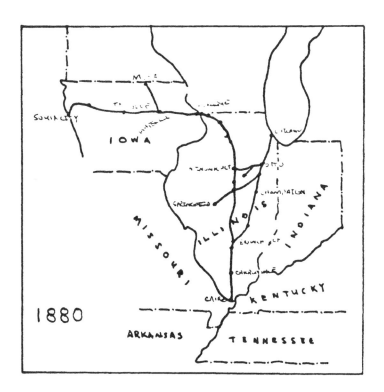

Based on Stover, Illinois Central, p. 199 and Butterbaugh, Atlas of Traffic Maps, p. 145.

APPENDIX D:4 (continued)

ILLINOIS CENTRAL 1890

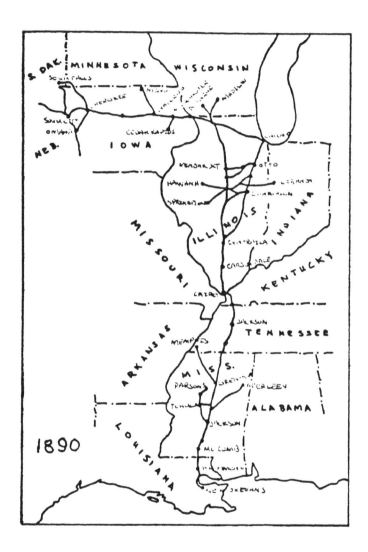

Based on Stover, Illinois Central, p. 203 and Butterbaugh, Atlas of Traffic Maps, p. 145.

APPENDIX D:4 (continued)

ILLINOIS CENTRAL 1900

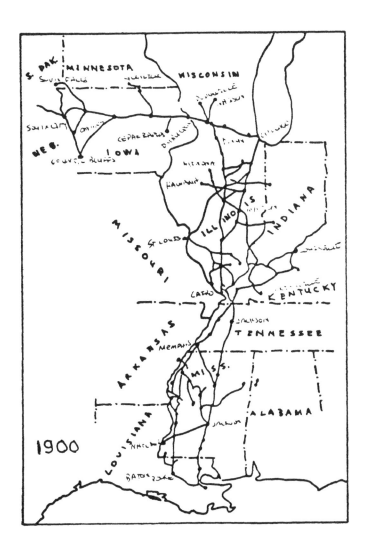

1900

Based on Stover, Illinois Central, p. 232 and Butterbaugh, Atlas of Traffic Maps, p. 145.

APPENDIX D:5

LOUISVILLE & NASHVILLE 1870

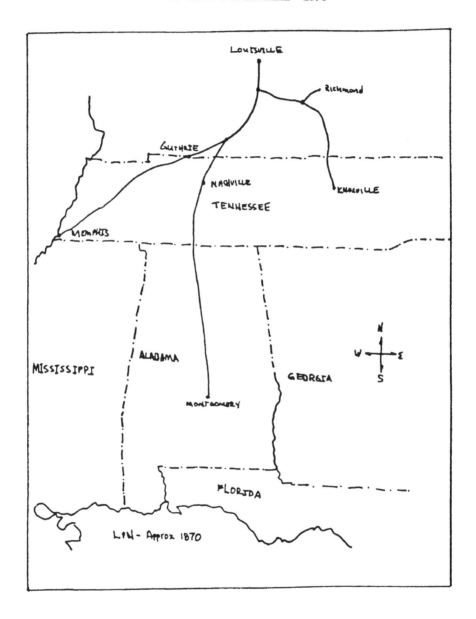

Based on Klein, Louisville and Nashville, p. 131 and Butterbaugh, Atlas of Traffic Maps, p. 147.

APPENDIX D:5 (continued)

LOUISVILLE & NASHVILLE 1880

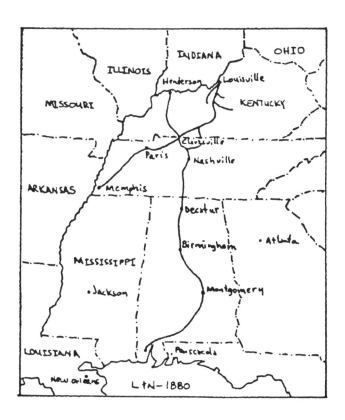

Based on Stover, Railroads of the South, p. 216 and Butterbaugh, Atlas of Traffic Maps, p. 147.

APPENDIX D:5 (continued)

LOUISVILLE & NASHVILLE 1890

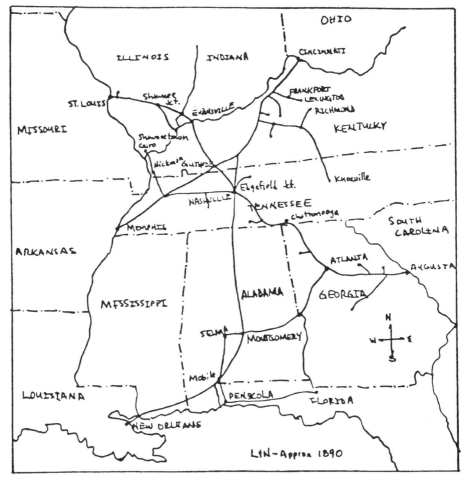

Based on Klein, _Louisville and Nashville_, p. 184 and Butterbaugh, _Atlas of Traffic Maps_, p. 147.

APPENDIX D:5 (continued)

LOUISVILLE & NASHVILLE 1900

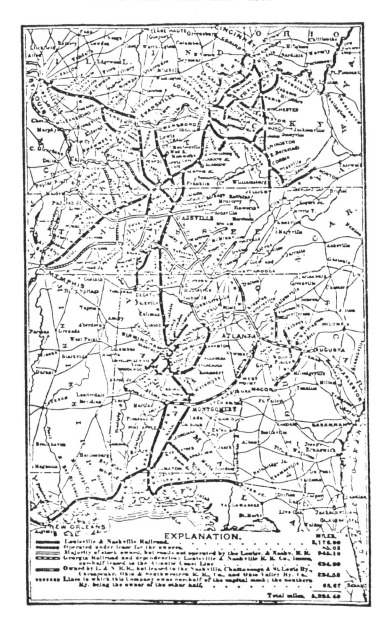

Source: <u>Poor's Manual of Railroads</u>, 1900, p. 409.

APPENDIX E

MILEAGE AND BACKGROUND OF SELECTED RAILROADS

APPENDIX E:1

Atchison, Topeka & Santa Fe Railway System

as of June 30, 1900

History: The Atchison, Topeka, and Santa Fe Railway System was orig-
inally chartered February 11, 1859, under the name of the Atchison and
Topeka Railroad Company. The name was changed on March 3, 1863 to
Atchison, Topeka, and Santa Fe Railroad Company and congressional land
grant transferred to the latter corporation. Construction began on
the main stem in 1869 with the whole line (470.58) miles completed and
opened February 20, 1873.

The Atchison, Topeka, and Santa Fe Railway System was incorporated
under the laws of Kansas on December 12, 1895, as successor to the
Atchison, Topeka, and Santa Fe Railroad Company whose property was sold
under foreclosure on December 10, 1895. Possession was taken on
January 1, 1896. The following depicts in detail the mileage of the
system as constituted as of June 30, 1900:

Atchison, Topeka and Santa Fe Ry.

	Miles
A. T. & S.F. Ry. proper (3,448.7 M)	
Corwith, Ill., to Kan. City, Mo. (inc. 6.44 m. leased)...	446.39
Ancona, Ill., to Pekin, Ill. (Inc. 5.91 m. leased).......	58.44
Lex. Jc. to St. Joe. & Win., Mo. (inc. 19.56 m. leased)..	96.01
Atchison, Kan., to Western Line of Kansas...............	470.41
Kansas City, Mo. to Topeka, Kan........................	66.04
Wilder to Cummings Junction, Kan.......................	45.41
Lawrence Junction to North Ottawa, Kan.................	26.52
North Ottawa to Emporia Junction, Kan..................	54.26
Burlington Junction to Burlington, Kan.................	41.47
Chanute to Pittsburg, Kan..............................	58.79
Cherryvale to Coffeyville, Kan.........................	17.98
Arkansas City, Kan., to Purcell Indian Ter.............	154.49
Wellington, Kan., to Tonkawa, O.T.....................	43.36
Attica to Medicine Lodge, Kan.........................	21.08
Holiday, Kan., to Ind. Ter. & Tex. State Line..........	442.21
Niotaze, Kan., to Owasso, I.T. (inc. 6.61 m. leased).....	64.40
Hutchison, Kan., to Ponca City, O.T....................	142.29

Source: Poor's Manual of Railroads, 1900, pp. 452-53.

APPENDIX E:1 - continued

	Miles
Wichita to Pratt, Kan.	79.77
Burlingame to Alma, Kan.	34.30
Kansas State Line to Pueblo & Pueblo Loop, Col.	150.05
Pueblo to Cannon City, Col.	40.23
La Junta, Col, to New Mexico State Line	96.32
Pueblo to Denver, Col.	116.33
New Mexico State Line to San Marcial, N.M.	353.80
San Marcial to Deming, N.M.	128.08
Rincon, N.M. to Texas State Line	56.74
Lamy to Santa Fe., N.M.	18.13
Deming to Silver City, N.M.	47.46
White Water to San Jose, N.M.	14.53
San Jose to Santa Rita, N.M.	4.28
Hanover to Fierro, N.M.	6.66
Socorro to Magdalena, N.M.	27.39
Nutt to Lake Valley, N.M.	13.52
Las Vegas to Hot Springs, N.M.	8.09
Dillon to Blossburg, N.M.	3.47

A. T. & S. F. Ry. in Chicago:
Chicago to Corwith, Ill.	6.43

Kansas City, Emporia and Southern Ry:
Emporia to Moline, Kan.	83.23

Florence, Eldorado and Walnut Valley R.R.:
Florence to Winfield, Kan.	72.73

Marion and McPherson, R.R.:
Florence to Ellinwood, Kan.	98.21

Wichita and Southwestern Ry. (115.18 M):
Newton to Arkansas City, Kan.	78.17
Mulvane to Caldwell, Kan.	37.01

Eastern Oklahoma Ry:
Guthrie to Pawnee, O.T.	71.58

Chicago, Kansas and Western R.R. (889.77 m.):
Osage City to Quenemo, Kan.	19.42
Gladstone, Kan., to Superior, Neb. (2.53 m. leased)	159.37
Abilene to Saline, Kan.	22.56
Manchester to Barnard, Kan.	43.56
Ellinore to Bazar, Kan.	6.67
Little River to Holyrood, Kan.	26.30
Augusta to Mulvane, Kan.	20.41
Mulvane, Kan., to East Line of Clark Co., Kan.	138.04
Hutchison to Kinsley, Kan.	83.56
Great Bend to Scott, Kan.	120.07

APPENDIX E:1 (continued)

	Miles
Larned to Jetmore, Kan.	46.33
Burlington to Gridley, Kan.	10.89
Colony to Yates Centre, Kan.	24.71
Chanute to Longton, Kan.	44.18
Benedict to Madison Junc., Kan.	40.57
Independence to Cedarvale, Kan.	54.79
East Line Clark Co. to Englewood, Kan.	28.34

Rio Grande and El Paso R.R.:

New Mexico Line to El Paso, Tex.	20.17

Total............4,806.00

Southern Kansas Ry. of Texas

Texas State Line to Panhandle City, Tex.	100.41
Panhandle City to Washburn, Tex.	14.72
Washburn to Amarillo, Tex. (leased)	14.04

Total............ 129.17

Gulf, Colorado and Santa Fe Ry.

Galveston, Tex., to Purcell, Ind. Ter.	518.67
Alvin to Houston, Tex.	25.66
Somerville to Conroe, Tex.	73.62
Conroe to end of track	29.62
Temple to San Angelo, Tex.	229.28
Coleman Junction to Coleman, Tex.	6.28
Cleburne to Dallas, Tex.	53.46
Dallas to Paris, Tex.	100.90
Ladonia to Honey Grove, Tex.	11.72
Cleburne to Weatherford, Tex.	39.90
Wolfe City to Sherman, Tex. (leased)	38.70

Total 1,127.81

Southern California Ry.

Barstow to National City, Cal.	200.08
San Bernardine to Los Angeles, Cal.	59.97
Los Angeles to Los Angeles Junc., Cal.	83.02
Highgrove to Orange, Cal.	40.78
Perris to San Jacinto, Cal.	19.44
Escondido Junction to Escondido, Cal.	21.30
San Bernadine to Highland Junc., Cal.	25.39
Redondo Junc. to Santa Monica, Cal.	18.86
Inglewood to Redondo, Cal.	10.77
Elsinore Junc. to Alberhill, Cal.	7.76
Total	487.37

APPENDIX E:1 (continued)

Santa Fe Pacific R.R.

	Miles
Isleta, N.M., to Needles, Cal............................	563.01
Needles to Mojave, Cal. (leased)........................	242.61
Mojave to Kern Junction, Cal............................	67.28
Kern Junction to Bakersfield, Cal.......................	2.40
Total...	875.30

RECAPITULATION:

Atchison, Topeka & Santa Fe Ry.........................	4,935.17
Gulf, Colorado & Santa Fe Ry...........................	1,127.81
Southern California Ry.................................	487.37
Santa Fe Pacific R.R...................................	875.30
Grand Total, Atchison System...........................	7,425.65

APPENDIX E:2

Boston & Maine Railroad

as of June 30, 1900

History: The Boston and Maine Railroad was formed by various consolidations; the most recent consolidation being May 9, 1890, and compris-
ing the Boston and Maine, the Eastern, and the Portsmouth, Great Falls
and Conway Railroad Companies. The Boston and Maine was chartered in
New Hampshire on June 27, 1835 and through leases, consolidations,
or stock ownership ocquired the following mileage as of June 30, 1900:

Main Lines Owned:
Boston, Mass., to Portland, Me., Western Div............115.31 miles
Boston, Mass., to Portland, Me., Eastern Div............108.29 "
Conway Junc., Me., to Intervale Junc., N.H.............. 73.37 "
Portland, Me., to Rochester, N.H. (P. & R. RR.)......... 53.86 "

Saugus Branch: Everett to Lynn, Mass........... 9.55 m.
Lawrence Branch: Salem to North Andover, Mass.. 19.89 m.
South Reading Branch: Peabody to Wakefield,Mass. 8.12 m.
Gloucester Branch: Beverly to Rockport, Mass....16.94 m.
Essex Branch: Wenham to Essex, Mass. .... 6.00 m.
Dover and Winnipiseogee Branch: Dover to
  Alton Bay, N.H................................29.00 m.
Wolfeborough Branch: Sanbornville to
  Wolfeborough, N.H...........................12.03 m.
Portsmouth and Dover Branch: Portsmouth to
  Dover, N. H...................................10.88 m.
Portsmouth Electric Ry: Portsmouth to
  Rye Beach, N. H...............................16.47 m.
Other Branches: Medford, 2 m., Methuen, 3.75 m.;
West Amesbury, 4.45 m.; Orchard Beach, 3.27 m.;
Charlestown, 1.09 m.; East Boston, 3.47 m.;
Chelsea Beach, 3.34 m.; Swampscott, 3.96 m.;
Marblehead, 3.52 m.; Asbury Grove, 1.06 m.;
Newburyport City, 1.97 m.; Salisbury, 3.79 m.;
Somersworth, 2.75 m.; Lowell and Lawrence
and Lowell and Andover Connection, Lowell
(0.37 m. of double track, of which 0.12 m.
of single track is owned by L.&A. RR.), 0.25 m.;
Union (Portland), 1.12 m.....................39.79 m.-168.67 "

Source: Poor's Manual of Railroads, 1900, pp. 4 and 8.

APPENDIX E:2 (continued

	Miles
Leased Lines...1,267.54	''

Total length of all lines operated (owned, 519.50 m.),
June 20, 1900.....................................1,787.04 miles

LEASED LINES:

NAME OF ROAD	FROM	TO	MILES
Danvers RR..............Wakefield Jc.,Mass.Danvers, Mass......			9.26
Newburyport RR.........Bradford..........Newb'p&Dv.,Mass....			26.98
Lowell and Andover RR...Lowell, Mass......Lowell Jc., Mass...			8.85
Kenneb'k & Kenneb'kpt RR.In Kenneb'kport,Ma..................			4.50
Boston & Lowell RR. & Brs. See Page 8*......................			96.95
Nashua & Lowell RR.....Lowell, Mass......Nashua, N.H........			14.50
Ct.&Passumpsic Rys.RR..White River Js.,Vt.Canada-Vt. Line....			110.30
Massawippi V'y Ry.& Br.See Page 9*..........................			35.46
Grand Trunk(trackage)..Lennoxville, P.Q...Sherbrooke, P.Q....			2.95
Central Mass. RR.......No. Camb'ge Jc.,Mass.Northhampton, Mass			98.77
Stony Brook RR.........No. Chelmsf'd,Mass.Ayer, Mass.........			13.16
Wilton RR..............Nashua, N.H.......Wilton, N.H........			15.50
Peterborough RR........Wilton, N.H...... .Greenfield, N.H....			10.50
Manchester & Keene RR..Keene, N.H...... Greenfield, N.H....			29.59
Worcester,Nas.&R'ch'rRR.Worcester, Mass....Rochester, N.H.....			94.48
Northern RR. & Brs......See Page 11*.......................			82.91
Peterb'gh&Hillsboro'RR.Peterborough,N.H...Hillsboro'Br., N.H.			18.51
C. & C.(N.H.) RR. & Br.See Page 12*........................			70.90
Manchester & LawrenceRR.Manchester, N.H....Massachusetts Line.			22.39
Connecticut River RR....Springfield, Mass..Keene, N.H. & Brs..			79.85
Concord & Montr'l RR&Brs.See Page 10*........................			209.61
Nash,Acton&Boston RR...Nashua, N.H.......North Acton, Mass..			20.12
N.Y.,N.H.&H.RR(tr'k'ge)North Acton, Mass..Concord Junc.,Mass.			4.21
Manch.& No.Weare RR....Manchester, N.H...Henniker, N.H......			24.50
Lake Shore RR.........Lakeport, N.H......Alton Bay, N.H.....			17.28
Tilton & Belmont RR....Belmont Jc.,N.H...Belmont, N.H.......			4.17
Whitef'd& Jeff. RR.&Brs.See Page11*.........................			33.69
Profile& Frac.Notch RR.Profile House,N.H..Bethlehem, N.H.....			12.84
Franklin & Tilton RR...Tilton, N.H.......Franklin Jc., N.H..			4.95
New Boston RR.........Parkers, N.H......New Boston, N.H....			5.19
Concord&Portsmouth RR..Manchester, N.H....Portsm'h,N.H.,·& Spr.39.87			
Suncook Valley RR......Suncook, N.H......Pittsfield, N.H......17.41			
Suncook Valley Ext.....Pittsfield, N.H....Centre Barnstead..... 4.46			
Pemigewasset Valley RR.Plymouth, N.H.....Lincoln, N.H........22.93			
Fitchburg RR. & Brs.....See Page 12*.........................393.94			
Troy & Bennington RR...Hoosac Junc., N.Y..Vermont State Line.. 5.04			
Vermont and Mass. RR...See Page 12*.......................... 58.80			

APPENDIX E:3

Chicago, Burlington & Quincy

as of June 30, 1900

History: The Chicago, Burlington, and Quincy Railroad was chartered as the Aurora Branch Railroad Company on February 12, 1949. The name was changed to Chicago and Aurora Railroad Company on June 22, 1852 and to its present corporate title on February 14, 1855. By one or other of the above companies was built the section of main line from Chicago to Mendota, Illinois, 76.89 miles and the branch from Aurora to West Chicago, Illinois, 12.35 miles. The rest of the mileage both east and west of the Missouri River, was acquired from time to time by purchases at foreclosure sales, by consolidations, and especially by construction under the charters of various proprietary companies. The following depicts in detail the mileage of the system as constituted as of January 1, 1900:

Lines Owned Absolutely

East of Missouri River

C., B. & Q. RR. (2618.91 m.):	Miles
Chicago, Ill., to Pacific Junction, Ia........	480.48
Galesburg to Quincy, Ill.....................	100.05
Loop Line at Quincy, Ill.....................	1.78
Aurora to West Chicago, Ill..................	12.35
Geneva to Streator, Ill......................	67.25
South Aurora to Portage Curve, Ill..........	134.71
East Dubuque, Ill., to Minneapolis, Minn.....	244.84
Oregon to Forreston, Ill....................	17.93
Flag Center to Rockford, Ill................	23.50
Galena Junction to Galena, Ill..............	3.82
Main Track in Dubuque, Ia...................	0.53
Main Track in East Winona, Wis..............	0.14
Main Track in Winona, Minn..................	1.20
Sheridan to Paw Paw, Ill....................	19.54
Shreator to Walnut, Ill.....................	58.76
Shabbona to Sterling, Ill..................	47.98
Mendota via E. Clinton to Savanna, Ill........	81.73
Main Track in East Clinton, Ill.............	0.34
Buda to Elmwood, Ill........................	44.51

Source: Poor's Manual of Railroads, 1900, pp. 216-17.

APPENDIX E:3 (continued)

	Miles
Yates City to Rushville, Ill	62.79
Galva to New Boston, Ill	50.63
Arpee to Keithsburg, Ill	6.25
Gladstone to Keithsburg, Ill	17.13
Galesburg to Peoria, Ill	52.77
Galesburg to Rio, Ill	12.22
Carthage Junction to Quincy, Ill	70.20
Quincy to East Louisiana, Ill	41.69
Fall Creek to East Hannibal, Ill	4.67
Rock Island via Monmouth to Wann, Ill	227.54
Main Track in East Alton, Ill	0.17
Barstow to Sterling, Ill	40.44
Burlington to Keokuk, Ia	42.33
Albia to Des Moines, Ia	67.94
Chariton to Indianola, Ia	33.16
Chariton, Ia. to St. Joseph, Mo	143.14
Bethany Junction, Ia., to Albany, Mo	65.54
Van Wert to Shenandoah, Ia	95.45
Creston to Cumberland, Ia	47.83
Creston, Ia. to Hopkins, Mo	42.75
Villisca, Ia., to Burlington Junction, Mo	35.00
Clarinda to Northboro, Ia	15.89
Red Oak to Griswold, Ia	18.04
Red Oak to Hamburg, Ia	39.17
Hastings to Carson, Ia	15.79
Hastings to Sidney, Ia	21.12
"Y" Track at Pacific Junction, Ia	0.39
Main Track in Council Bluffs, Ia	1.57
Napier, Mo., to Rulo Bridge Junction	5.86

Hannibal and St. Joseph RR. (289.22 m.):	
Hannibal to St. Joseph, Mo	206.52
Palmyra Junction to West Quincy, Mo	12.65
Cameron Junction to Kansas City, Mo	54.16
St. Joseph to Rushville, Mo	15.34
Between Rushv., Mo., & Un. Depot,	
Atchison, Kan	0.55

K. C., St. J. & C. B. RR. (310.85 m.):	
Harlem, Mo., to Council Bluffs, Ia	189.37
Through Kansas City Yard	0.44
East Leavenworth to Stillings, Mo	1.05
Armour to Winthorp, Mo	2.96
Amazonia to State Line, Mo	52.30
Bigelow to Burlington Junction, Mo	31.54
Corning, Mo., to Northboro, Ia	29.54
Nebraska City Junction to Crosby, Ia	3.65

APPENDIX E:3 (continued)

St. L., K. & N. W. RR. (225.71 m.);   Miles
Keokuk, Ia., to West Quincy, Mo.............. 36.66
Moody to Hannibal, Mo........................ 13.25
Hannibal to Louisiana, Mo.................... 25.32
Louisiana to Franklin St., St. Louis, Mo..... 91.51
Cuivre Junction to St. Peters, Mo............ 10.55
Keokuk to Mt. Pleasant Junction, Ia.......... 47.96
Main Track in West Alton, Mo................. 0.46

C., B. & K. C. Ry. (181.56 m.):
Viele to Bloomfield Junction, Ia............. 59.79
Moulton, Ia., to Carrolton, Mo...............121.77

Keokuk and Western RR. (253.47 m.):
Alexandria, Mo., to Van Wert, Ia.............142.80
Des Moines, Ia., to Cainsville, Mo...........110.67

C., Ft. M. & D. M. RR.:
Keokuk to Ottumwa, Ia....................... 70.60

West of Missouri River

B. & M. R. RR. in Neb. (1,660.66 m.):
Pacific Junction, Ia., to Kearney, Neb...... 195.29
Aurora, Neb., to Colorado State Line........ 267.16
Lester to Table Rock, Neb................... 142.84
York to Central City, Neb................... 41.34
Nemaha to Salem, Neb........................ 17.60
Aurora, Neb., to Huntley, Mont.............. 751.21
Beatrice to Wymore, Neb..................... 11.87
Nemaha to Beatrice, Neb..................... 65.20
Edgemont to Deadwood, S.D................... 106.40
Englewood to Spearfish, S.D................. 31.91
Hill City Junction to Keystone, S.D......... 13.34
Minnekahta to Hot Springs, S.D.............. 9.50
Newcastle to Cambria, Wyo................... 7.00

Proprietary Railroads

West of Missouri River

Omaha and Southwestern RR.:
Omaha to Oreapolis, Neb..................... 16.88
Crete to Beatrice, Neb...................... 30.09

Nebraska Ry.:
Nemaha to York, Neb......................... 135.74
Nebraska City Bridge Line................... 2.12

APPENDIX E:3 (continued

	Miles
Atchison and Nebraska RR.:	
Atchison, Kan., to Lincoln, Neb..............	144.95
Rulo, Neb., to Rulo Bridge Junction.........	3.42
Lincoln and Northwestern RR.:	
Lincoln to Columbus, Neb...................	73.49
Burlington and Colorado RR.:	
Nebraska State Line to Denver, Co..........	174.89
Nebraska and Colorado RR.:	
DeWitt, Neb., to Colorado State Line........	298.32
Kenesaw to Oxford, Neb......................	60.67
Fairmont to Chester, Neb...................	45.19
Edgar to Superior, Neb.....................	26.53
Chicago, Nebraska and Kansas RR.:	
Odell, Neb., to Concordia, Kan..............	71.04
Republican Valley, Kansas and Southwestern RR.:	
Republican, Neb., to Oberlin, Kan...........	78.23
Omaha and North Platt RR.:	
Omaha to Schuyler, Neb.....................	80.59
Lincoln and Black Hills RR.:	
Central City to Ericson, Neb................	62.94
Palmer to Sargent, Neb.....................	73.29
Greeley Centre to Burwell, Neb..............	40.38
Oxford and Kansas RR.:	
Orleans, Neb., to Kansas State Line.........	59.6_
Beaver Valley RR.:	
Nebraska State Line to St. Francis, Kan......	74.18
Colorado and Wyoming RR.:	
Nebraska State Line to Wyoming State Line....	144.58
Cheyenne and Burlington RR.:	
Colorado State Line to Cheyenne, Wyo........	29.01
Denver, Utah and Pacific RR.:	
Denver to Utah Junction, Col................	3.00
Burns Junction to Lyons, Col...............	32.67

Republican Valley and Wyoming RR.:

APPENDIX E:3 (continued)

	Miles
Culbertson to Imperial, Neb.................	49.17

Nebraska, Wyoming and Western RR.:
| Alliance, Neb., to Colorado State Line...... | 87.08 |
| Northport, Neb., to Guernsey, Wyo........... | 94.78 |

Denver and Montana RR.:
| Brush to Union, Co.......................... | 11.39 |
| Sterling, Col, to Nebraska Line............. | 27.85 |

Trackage Rights

East of Missouri River

Pennsylvania Company:
| Depot to 16th St., Chicago, Ill.............. | 1.22 |

Chicago and Northwestern Ry.:
| East Clinton, Ill., to Clinton, Ia.......... | 1.06 |

Illinois Central RR.:
| Portage Curve to East Dubuque, Ill........... | 12.78 |
| East Dubuque to Dunleith & Dub. Bridge....... | 0.46 |

Dunleith and Dubuque Bridge:
| Mississippi River, Dubuque, Ia.............. | 0.66 |

St. Paul Union Depot:
| At St. Paul, Minn........................... | 0.53 |

Great Northern Ry.:
| Minneapolis to St. Paul, Minn............... | 11.65 |

Minneapolis Union Ry.:
| At Minneapolis, Minn........................ | 2.21 |

Winona Bridge Ry.:
| East Winona, Wis., to Winona, Minn.......... | 0.98 |

Quincy Bridge:
| Quincy, Ill., and West Quincy, Mo........... | 1.43 |

C., C., C. & St. L. Ry.:
| Warm to East St. Louis, Ill................. | 19.05 |
| East Alton to Alton, Ill.................... | 3.25 |

St. C., M. & St. L. Belt RR.:

APPENDIX E:3 (continued)

	Miles
Alton, Ill., to Bellefontaine Junction, Mo...	3.15

St. L. Ter. RR. & St. L. Mers'. Br.Ter. RR.:
At St. Louis, Mo.............................. 3.88

Chicago and Alton RR.:
East Louisiana, Ill., to Louisiana, Mo...... 2.41

Wabash RR.:
East Hannibal, Ill. to Hannibal, Mo........ 1.16
Moulton to Bloomsfield Junction, Ia........ 14.11

M. K. & T. Ry. H. B. & H. U. Depot:
At Hannibal, Mo.............................. 0.89

A. Un. Depot & RR. Co. & A. & E. Br. Co.:
Winthrop, Mo., to Atchison Union Depot...... 0.52

Leavenworth Terminal Ry. and Bridge:
Stillings, Mo., to Leavenworth, Kan........ 1.73

Keokuk and Hamilton Bridge:
At Keokuk, Ia............................... 0.03

Chicago, Milwaukee and St. Paul Ry.:
At Ottumwa, Ia.............................. 0.53

Kansas City Union Depot:
At Kansas City, Mo.......................... 0.41

West of Missouri River

Northern Pacific Ry1:
Huntley to Billings, Mont................... 12.62

Colorado and Southern Ry.:
Utah Junction to Burns Junction, Co........ 11.30

Union Pacific RR.:
Sterling to Union, Col..................... 23.50

RECAPITULATION

Mileage owned--C., B. & Q. RR..............2,618.91
B. & M. R. RR. in Neb.......1,660.66
H. & St. J. RR.............. 289.22
K. C., St. J. & C. B. RR.... 310.85
St. L., K. & N. W. RR....... 225.71

APPENDIX E:3 (continued

	Miles	
C., B. & K. C. Ry	181.56	
K. & W. RR	253.47	
C., Ft. M. & D. M. RR	70.60--5,610.98	

Mileage of Proprietary (leased) Railroads........ 2,032.08
Mileage of Trackage Rights....................... 131.52

Total Mileage, Jan. 1, 1901.................. 7,774.58

APPENDIX E:4

Illinois Central Railroad Company

as of June 30, 1900

History: The Illinois Central Railroad Company was chartered on February 10, 1851. The Dubuque, Iowa line was opened on June 11, 1855, through to Cairo, Illinois on September 27, 1856. All the lines of railroad operated by the company in connection with its main lines are controlled by it, nominally under leases or through stock ownership, but are practically parts of the Illinois Central property. For this reason no separate statements of the following lines were published separately in Poor's Manual. The following depicts in detail the mileage of the system as constituted as of June 30, 1900

Illinois Central RR. (705.50 m.):   Miles
  Centralia, Ill., to Dubuque, Ia.......... 364.73
  Chicago Div., Chicago to Cairo, Ill...... 340.77

South Chicago Branch:
  Parkside to South Chicago, Ill........... 4.76

Blue Island RR:
  Kensington to Blue Line, Ill............. 3.96

Mound City Ry.:
  Mound City Junction to Mound City, Ill..... 2.87

Kankakee & Southwestern RR. (131.26 m.):
  Otto to Normal Junction, Ill.............. 79.46
  Kempton Junc. to Kankakee Junc., Ill...... 41.80
  Buckingham to Tracy, Ill................. 10.00

Rantoul RR.:
  West Lebanon, Ind., to Leroy, Ill........ 74.40

Chicago and Springfield RR.:
  Gilman to Springfield, Ill...............111.47

Litchfield Division (St. L., P. & N. Ry.):
  Springfield to East St. Louis, Ill........ 97.59

Source: Poor's Manual of Railroads, 1900, p. 257.

APPENDIX E:4 (continued)

Chicago, Havana & Western RR. (131.62 m.):   Miles
  Havana to Champaign, Ill.................. 100.58
  White Heath to Decator, Ill............... 31.04

Effingham District (St. L., I & E RR.):
  Effingham, Ill., to Switz City, Ind....... 88.51

Chicago, Madison & Northern RR. (231.30 m.):
  Freeport, Ill., to Madison, Wis........... 61.80
  Cedarville Junc., Ill. to Dodgeville, Wis.. 57.36
  Freeport, Ill., to Clarke St., Chicago..... 112.14

St. Louis Div., St. L., A. & T.H. RR. (239.04 m.):
  East St. Louis to Eldorado, Ill........... 121.00
  Bellevue to East Carondelet, Ill.......... 17.30
  Pinckneyville to Brooklyn, Ill............ 98.43
  Harrison to Murphysboro, Ill..............   2.31

Chicago and Texas RR. (79 m):
  Johnston City to East Cape Girardeau, Ill... 73.00
  Mobile Junction to Garrison Shaft........... 2.00
  McClure to Gale, Ill........................ 4.00

    Total Northern Lines...................1,901.28

Dubuque & Sioux City RR. (730.61 m):
  Dubuque to Sioux City, Ia................. 326.58
  Onawa, Ia., to Sioux Falls, S.D........... 155.58
  Cedar Rapids to Manchester, Ia............ 41.85
  Cedar Falls Junc., Ia., to Lyle, Minn. Line 75.58
  Tara to Council Bluffs, Ia................ 131.02

Stacyville RR.:
  Near Lyle, Minn., to Stacyville, Ia.......   7.66

    Total Western Lines.................... 738.27

Chic., St. L. & New Orleans RR. (664.99 m):
  Cairo, Ill., to Canton, Miss.............. 341.03
  Canton, Miss., to New Orleans, La......... 206.76
  Memphis Div., Grenada to Memphis, Tenn.... 100.00
  Durant to Kosciusko, Miss................. 17.20

Louisville Div., C., St. L. & N. O. RR. (578.72 m.):
  Memphis, Tenn., to Louisville, Ky......... 398.12
  Owensboro to Horse Branch, Ky............. 42.16
  Evansville, Ind., to Hopkinsville, Ky..... 128.94
  Morganfield to Uniontown, Ky.............   7.50

APPENDIX E:4 (continued)

	Miles
DeKoven, Ky., to Ohio River...............	2.00
Hodgenville and Elizabethtown Ry.: Hosgenville to Elizabethtown, Ky..........	11.10
Troy and Tiptonville RR.: Moffat to Troy, Tenn.....................	4.60
Canton, Aberdeen & Nashville RR.: Aberdeen to Kosciusko, Miss..............	89.06
Canton, Aberdeen & Nashville RR. in Ala.: Winfield to Brilliant, Ala...............	7.84
Total Southern Lines...................1,356.31	
Total of all Lines.....................3,995.86	

APPENDIX E:5

Louisville and Nashville

as of June 30, 1900

History: The Louisville and Nashville Railroad was chartered on March 5, 1850 by Act of the Kentucky legislature. The main stem was opened on November 1, 1859 with other lines added to the system from time to time as depicted below:

Lines of Road.--I. OWNED ABSOLUTELY OR THROUGH OWNERSHIP OF THE ENTIRE CAPITAL STOCK

Main Stem: Louisville, Ky., to Nashville, Tenn...........185.92 miles
Nash., Florence & Sheff. Ry.: Columbia to
    Sheffield, Ala........................ 82.13
West Point Branch: Iron City to
    Pinkney,Ala........................... 11.78
Napier Branch: Summertown to Napier, Ala. 10.92
Sheffield & Tuscumbia RR.: Sheffield
    to Tuscumbia, Ala..................... 2.63--107.46 m.
Montgomery & Prattville RR.: Prattville
    Jc. to Prattville, Ala................   10.35 m.
Birmingham Mineral RR. (See subjoined state-
    ment therefor)........................   162.86 m.
Alabama Mineral RR. (See subjoined state-
    ment therefor)........................   133.88 m.
Mobile and Montgomery Ry.: Montgomery to
    Mobile, Ala...........................   178.49 m.
New Orleans and Mobile RR.: Mobile, Ala, to
    New Orleans, La.......................   140.36 m.
Pontchartrain RR.: Pontchartrain Junction to
    Milneburg, La.........................   5.18 m.
Bardstown Branch: Bardstown Junction to
    Bardstown, Ky.........................   17.37 m.
Springfield Branch: Bardstown, Ky., to
    Springfield, Ky.......................   20.07 m.
Knoxville Branch: Lebanon Junction to Jellico,
    Tenn..................................   171.17 m.
Cumberland Valley Branch: Corbin, Ky., to
    Norton, Va............................   117.37 m.

Source: Poor's Manual of Railroads, 1900, pp. 408 and 410.

APPENDIX E:5 (continued)

Middlesborough RR.: Middlesborough to Coal Mines, Tenn....................		9.96 m.
Memphis Line: Memphis Junction to Memphis, Tenn................................		259.13 m.
Owensboro & Nashville Ry. (See subjoined Statement)...........................		88.10 m.
Clarksville and Princeton Branch: Princeton Jc. to Gracey, Tenn...................		32.00 m.

Clarksville Mineral Branch:

Hematite to Pond, Tenn.....	32.03	
Van Leer to Cumberl'd Furn.	9.00--	38.03 m.

Henderson Division:

Edgefield Jc. to Henderson, Ky.	134.76	

Madisonville Branch:

Madisonville to Providence, Ky.	16.10--	150.86 m.
Southeast & St. Louis RR. (See subjoined statement)....................		208.74 m.
Southern Alabama RR.: Gulf Junc. to Escambia Junc., Ala..................		109.29 m.
Pensacola Division: Flomaton, Ala, to Pensacola, Fla........................		44.40 m.
Pensacola and Atlantic RR.: Pensacola to River Junction, Fla....................		160.14 m.

Cincinnati Division: Louisville to

Newport, Ky....................	109.70	

Louisville Ry. Transfer: E. Louis-

ville to S. Louisville, Ky.....	4.13--	113.83 m.

Lexington Branch: LaGrange to

Lexington, Ky..................	67.00	

Shelby Cut-off: Shelbyville to

Christiansburg, Ky.............	8.51--	75.51 m.
Louisville, H.C. & Westport RR.: Louisville to Prospect, Ky..............		11.16 m.
Kentucky Central Ry. (See subjoined statement therefor)....................		247.65 m.-- 2,613.36 Miles

Total..2,799.28 Miles

II. LINE OVER WHICH THIS COMPANY RUNS ITS TRAINS, THE EARNINGS OF WHICH ACCRUE TO THIS COMPANY.

Birmingham Mineral RR.: Gurnee Junc. to Blocton, Ala....14.41 miles

III. OPERATED UNDER LEASE--EARNINGS IN EXCESS OF FIXED CHARGES ACCRUING TO THIS COMPANY.

APPENDIX E:5 (continued)

Nashville and Decatur RR.: Nashville, Tenn.
    to Decatur, Ala.......................... 119.24 m.
Shelby RR.: Anchorage, Ky., to Shelbyville,
    Ky...................................... 19.10 m.-- 138.34 miles

IV. OPERATED FOR ACCOUNT SO. & NO. ALA. RR. CO.

So. and No. Ala. RR.: New Decatur, Ala., to
    Montgomery, Ala.......................... 182.67 m.
Wetumpka Branch: Elmore, Ala. to
    Wetumpka, Ala............................ 6.30 m.-- 188.97 miles

    Total Louisville and Nashville System............... 3,141.00 miles

V.--OPERATED UNDER LEASE FOR ACCOUNT OF THE VARIOUS COMPANIES

Cumberland & Ohio RR. (So.Div.): Cumb. & Ohio
    Jc. to Gr'nb'g, Ky...................... 30.90 m.
Glasgow RR.: Junc. (90 m. s. w. Louisville)
    to Glascow, Ky.......................... 10.50 m.
Elkton and Guthrie RR.: Elkton Junc., Ky.,
    to Elkton, Ky........................... 10.92 m.
Alabama and Florida RR.: Georgiana to
    Andalusia, Ala.......................... 32.71 m.-- 85.03 "

VI. LINES OUTSIDE OF ITS OWN SYSTEM IN WHICH L. & N. CO.
IS INTERESTED AS OWNER OF MAJORITY OF STOCK.

Nashville, Chattanooga and St. Louis, Ry.
    (See GENERAL INDEX)..................... 935.12 m.
Henderson Bridge and Connecting track,
    (See appended statement)................ 10.06 m.-- 945.18 miles

VII. LINES IN WHICH THE COMPANY IS INTERESTED AS LESSEE.

Georgia RR., and dependencies. (See GENERAL INDEX).... 624.00 "

VIII. LINES IN WHICH THIS COMPANY OWNS ONE-HALF OF THE
CAPITAL STOCK. THE SOUTHERN RY. CO. BEING THE
OWNER OF THE OTHER HALF.

Birmingham Southern RR.: In the State of
    Alabama................................. 68.00 m.
Central Transfer Ry. and Storage Co.: In
    Louisville, Ky.......................... 0.67 m.-- 68.67 "

IX. LINES OWNED BUT NOT OPERATED BY THE COMPANY.

APPENDIX E:5 (continued)

Paducah and Memphis Div.: Memphis, Tenn., to
  Paducah, Ky............................... 245.20 m.
Cecilia Branch: Louisville, Ky. to
  Cecilia Junc............................. 46.00 m.
Clarksville and Princeton Br.: Gracey to
  Princeton, Ky........................... 20.70 m.--320.90 Miles

   X.   LINE OWNED BY THIS COMPANY--EARNINGS OF WHICH ACCRUE
       TO S. & N. A. RR. CO.

New and Old Decatur Belt and Terminal Co.....   3.62 miles

Total length of all lines owned, operated, and
  controlled, June 30, 1900........................ 5,188.40 miles

APPENDIX F

PRESIDENTS OF SELECTED RAILROADS

APPENDIX F:1

PRESIDENTS

Atchison, Topeka & Santa Fe*

President	From	To
Cyrus K. Holliday	November 2, 1863	January 13, 1864
S. C. Pomery	January 13, 1864	September 2, 1868
William F. Nast	September 2, 1868	September 24, 1868
Henry C. Lord	September 24, 1868	February 17, 1869
Henry Keyes	February 17, 1869	September 24, 1870
Ginery Twitchell	October 10, 1870	May 22, 1873
Henry Strong	May 22, 1873	May 28, 1874
Thomas Nickerson	May 28, 1874	May 13, 1880
T. Jefferson Collidge	May 13, 1880	August 1, 1881
William B. Strong	August 1, 1881	September 6, 1889
Allen Manuel	September 6, 1889	February 24, 1893
J. W. Reinhart	March 7, 1893	September 1, 1894
D. B. Robinson (acting)	September 1, 1894	December 12, 1895
Edward P. Ripley	December 12, 1895	January 1, 1920

---

*Source: Keith L. Bryant, Jr., History of the Atchison, Topeka and Santa Fe Railway (New York: Macmillan, 1974).

APPENDIX F:2

PRESIDENTS

Boston & Maine Railroad

President	From	To
Daniel M. Durell	August 1835	September 1836
Hobart Clark	September 1836	November 1841
Thomas West	November 1841	September 1849
John Howe	September 1849	September 1852
Southworth Shaw	September 1852	September 1853
James Haywood	September 1853	September 1856
Francis Cogswell	September 1856	September 1862
Israel Spelman	September 1862	September 1865
Francis Cogswell	October 1865	November 1871
Nathaniel G. White	November 1871	December 1881
George C. Lord	December 1881	December 1889
Frank Jones	December 1889	October 26, 1892
Archibald A. McLeod	October 26, 1892	May 23, 1893
Frank Jones	June 27, 1893	October 11, 1893
Lucius Tuttle	October 11, 1893	October 12, 1910

APPENDIX F:3

PRESIDENTS

Chicago, Burlington & Quincy*

President	From	To
Stephen Gale	February 22, 1849	February 21, 1851
Elisha Wadsworth	February 21, 1851	February 21, 1852
Stephen Gale	February 21, 1852	February 21, 1853
James F. Joy	February 21, 1853	June 12, 1857
John Van Nortwick	June 12, 1857	July 12, 1865
James F. Joy	July 12, 1865	July 11, 1871
James M. Walker	July 11, 1871	March 2, 1876
Robert Harris	March 2, 1876	May 25, 1878
J. M. Forbes	May 25, 1878	September 29, 1881
C. E. Perkins	September 29, 1881	March 1, 1901
George B. Harris	March 1, 1901	January 31, 1910

*Source: Richard C. Overton, Burlington Route: A History of the Burlington Lines (New York: Alfred A. Knopf, 1965).

APPENDIX F:4

PRESIDENTS

Illinois Central Railroad*

President	From	To
Robert Schuyler	1851	1853
William P. Burrall	1853	1854
John N. H. Griswold	1854	1855
William H. Osborn	1855	1865
John M. Douglas	1865	1871
John Newell	1871	1874
Wilson G. Hunt	1874	1875
John M. Douglas	1875	1877
William K. Ackerman	1877	1883
James C. Clarke	1883	1887
Stuyvesant Fish	1887	1906

---

*Source: John F. Stover, History of the Illinois Central Railroad (New York: Macmillan, 1975).

APPENDIX F:5

PRESIDENTS

Louisville & Nashville Railroad*

President	From	To
Levin L. Shreve	September 27, 1851	October 2, 1854
John L. Helm	October 2, 1854	October 2, 1860
James Guthrie	October 2, 1860	June 11, 1868
Russell Houston	June 11, 1868	October 8, 1868
H. D. Newcomb	October 8, 1868	August 18, 1874
Thomas J. Martin	August 18, 1874	October 6, 1875
E. D. Standiford	October 6, 1875	March 24, 1880
H. V. Newcomb	March 24, 1880	December 1, 1880
E. H. Green	December 1, 1880	February 26, 1881
Christopher C. Baldwin	February 26, 1881	May 19, 1884
J. S. Rogers	Mary 19, 1884	June 17, 1884
Milton H. Smith	June 17, 1884	October 6, 1886
Eckstein Norton	October 6, 1886	March 9, 1891
Milton H. Smith	March 9, 1891	February 22, 1921

---

*Source: Maury Klein, History of the Louisville and Nashville Railroad, (New York: MacmilIan, 1972).

APPENDIX G

SOME MATERIALS AVAILABLE TO

RAILROAD HISTORIANS

UNIVERSITY OF NEBRASKA-LINCOLN LIBRARIES

CHARLES J. KENNEDY RAILROAD COLLECTION*

1. Annual reports of all railroads in the United States to their stockholders. The collection at the University of Nebraska is incomplete but plans are to complete the file with a microfilm or life-size photocopy.

2. Annual reports from each railroad in the U.S. to the state legislature or railroad (or public utility) commission. The University of Nebraska-Lincoln now has the almost complete set of such reports which the Association of American Railroads sold to the University a few years ago. The University is now arranging to acquire copies or photocopies of the missing volumes.

3. Interstate Commerce Commission, Statistics of Railways in the United States, 1888-1953, and Transport Statistics: Annual Report, 1954 - the present. Complete set.

4. Replies by each railroad to the I.C.C. responding to Valuation Order 20 of May 13, 1915, which shows when and where each little piece of each railroad and each of its predecessors was built and who has owned, leased, and operated it to 1915. The Interstate Commerce Commission permitted the University of Nebraska-Lincoln to photocopy its incomplete collection. Professor Kennedy is now contacting each railroad for the missing reports.

5. The minutes of the directors and stockholders of each operating railroad in the U.S. until it was leased, merged or consolidated. The Union Pacific Railroad has donated all of its records to 1889, including the original copy of directors' and stockholders' minutes, to the Nebraska State Historical Society Archives, which is located only two blocks from the main library of the University of Nebraska-Lincoln. Arrangements are being made with other railroads for a microfilm or life-size photocopy of their minutes at the University of Nebraska-Lincoln main library with such restrictions, if any, each company may specify.

---

* For further information write to Prof. Charles Kennedy, College of Business Administration, University of Nebraska-Lincoln, Lincoln, Nebraska 68588. Phone 402-472-2325 or residence 402-488-0684.

6. **Freight** and **passenger** **tariffs** **of** **172** **railroads** **and** **their** **prede-cessors** **for** **1887-1891**, which the National Archives had saved **before** destroying the tariffs of the other railroads, and the full **set** of the tariffs of the Boston & Maine and Maine Central and **its** predecessors from 1887 to 1945. These tariffs were donated by **the** U.S. National Archives to the University of Nebraska-Lincoln. Tariffs and rate contracts before 1887 will be added. Contracts including division of rates also are being sought.

7. **Henry** V. Poor, **History** **of** the **Railroads** **and** **Canals** **of** the **U.S.A.** . . . (1860), and **Manual** **of** the **Railroads** **of** the **U.S.A.** , **1868-1924.** The set at the University of Nebraska-Lincoln is complete.

8. **All** **railroad** **weekly** **newspapers** **and** **monthly** **magazines** **printed** **in** **the** **United** **States**. The collection is almost complete; some are **original** issues, others are on microfilm.

9. **Miscellaneous** **documents** **and** **out-of-print** **volumes** **on** **railroads** **in** **the** **U.S**.

BIBLIOGRAPHY

BIBIOGRAPHY

Adler, Cyrus. Jacob H. Schiff: His Life and Letters. 2 vols. New York: Doubleday, Doran, 1929.

American Accounting Association Committee on Auditing Concepts. "A Statement of Basic Auditing Concepts." Accounting Review, suppl. to Vol. 47 (1972).

American Institute of Management. Appraising a Management. Pamphlet. Vol. 1, No. 21. New York: AIM, 1950.

------------. The Management Audit Bookshelf. 12 vols. New York: AIM, 1959.

------------. Manual of Excellent Managements. 10th ed. New York: AIM, 1966.

American Institute of Certified Public Accountants. Statement on Auditing Standards. No. 1, 1973.

Annual Reports of the Board of Directors of the Atchison, Topeka and Santa Fe Railroad Company to the Stockholders. Selected years, 1870-1901.

Annual Reports of the Board of Directors of the Boston and Maine Railroad Company to the Stockholders. Selected years, 1870-1901.

Annual Reports of the Board of Directors of the Chicago, Burlington and Quincy Railroad Company to the Stockholders. Selected years, 1870-1901.

Annual Reports of the Board of Directors of the Illinois Central Railroad to the Stockholders. Selected years, 1870-1901.

Annual Reports of the Board of Directors of the Louisville and Nashville Railroad Company to the Stockholders. Selected years, 1870-1901.

Argyris, Chris. Integrating the Individual and the Organization. New York: John Wiley & Sons, 1964.

Association of American Railroads, Committee on Costs and Statistics. Railway Statistics Manual. Washington: Association of American Railroads, 1964.

Atwood, Albert. "Sound Properties: The Atchison," Harper's Weekly, 59 (July 18, 1914), 71-72.

Baker, George P. The Formation of the New England Railroad System. Cambridge: Harvard University Press, 1949.

Beloit, Bruce W. "Appraisal of Management Competence As A Measurement in Economic and Business History Research." Unpublished Master's Thesis, University of Nebraska, 1967.

Boulding, Kenneth. "General Systems Theory: The Skeleton of Science." Management Science (April 1956), 197-208.

Bradlee, Francis C.B. The Boston and Maine Railroad: A History of the Maine Road, With Its Tributary Lines. Salem, MA: Essex Institute, 1921.

Bradley, Glen D. The Story of the Santa Fe. Boston: Gorham Press, 1920.

Bright, Arthur A., Jr. and George H. Ellis, eds. The Economic State of New England. New Haven: Yale University Press, 1954.

Bromage, Mary C. "Wording the Management Audit." The Journal of Accountancy, 133 (Feb. 1972), 50-57.

Bryant, Keith. History of the Atchison, Topeka and Santa Fe. New York: Macmillan, 1960.

Buchele, Robert B. "How to Evaluate a Firm." Californian Management Review (Fall 1962), 5-17.

Burnell, Edward H. Railway Accounting and Statistics. Chicago: Watson Publications, 1955.

Bures, Allen L. "The Management Approach in Writing Business History." A paper presented at the Symposium on Accounting and Management Appraisal in Writing Railroad History, Denver, April 29, 1978.

------------. "The Management Audit Approach in Writing Economic History." A paper presented at the North American Economic Studies Association, Mexico City, Mexico, Dec. 28, 1978.

Burton, John C. "Management Auditing." The Journal of Accountancy, 125 (May 1968), 41-46.

Carson, Clarence B. Throttling the Railroads. Indianapolis: Liberty Fund, 1971.

Cashin, James A., ed. Handbook for Auditors. New York: McGraw-Hill, 1971.

Cayley, M. A. "Marketing-Research Planning and Evaluation." The Business Quarterly, 40 (Spring 1975), 30-36.

Chamberlain, John. The Enterprising Americans: A Business History of the United States. New York: Harper & Row, 1963.

Chandler, Alfred D., Jr. The Railroads: The Nation's First Big Business. New York: Harcourt, Brace and World, 1965.

------------. The Visible Hand: The Managerial Revolution in American Business. Cambridge: Belknap Press of Harvard University Press, 1977.

Clark, Ira G. Then Came the Railroads. Norman, OK: University of Oklahoma Press, 1958.

Clark, P. A. Action Research and Organizational Change. New York: Harper and Row, 1972.

Clark, Thomas D. A Pioneer Southern Railroad from New Orleans to Cairo. Chapel Hill: University of North Carolina Press, 1936.

Cochran, Thomas C. Railroad Leaders, 1845-1890: The Business Mind In Action. Cambridge: Harvard University Press, 1953.

Cooley, Thomas M. The American Railway. New York: Charles Scribner's Sons, 1889.

Conly, George T. "Happiness is a Management Audit." The Journal of Accountancy, 135 (March 1973), 89-90.

Corliss, Carlton J. Main Line of Mid-America, The Story of the Illinois Central. New York: Creative Age Press, 1950.

Daggett, Stuart. Railroad Reorganization. Cambridge, MA: Harvard University Press, 1908.

Darr, Richard. A History of the Nashua and Lowell Rail-Road Corporation, 1835-1880. New York: Arno Press, 1976.

Davis, Keith, and Robert L. Blomstrom. Business and Society: Environment and Responsibility. New York: McGraw-Hill, 1975.

Derrick, Samuel Melanchthon. Centennial History of South Carolina Railroad. Columbia, SC: The State Company, 1930.

DeWitt, Frank. "Measuring Management Performance." Management Accounting (Nov. 1972), 18-22.

Dombrower, Denny. "The Professional Accountants Formula for Survival, Operational Auditing." Canadian Chartered Accountant, 101,

254

(Dec. 1972), 53.

Drucker, Peter F. An Introductory View of Management. New York: Harper & Row, 1977.

------------. Management: Tasks, Responsibilities, Practices. New York: Harper & Row, 1974.

------------. The New Society. New York: Harper & Row, 1950.

Dunnette, M. D., ed. Handbook of Industrial and Organizational Psychology. Chicago: Rand McNally, 1976.

Edds, John A. Auditing for Management. Toronto: Sir Isaac Pitman, 1971.

Emery, F. E. Systems Thinking. Baltimore: Penguin Books, 1962.

Fayol, Henri. Industrial and General Administration. Trans. J. A. Coubrough. Geneva: International Management Institute, 1930.

Fink, Henry T. Food and Flavor. New York: Century, 1913.

Gates, Paul W. The Illinois Central Railroad and Its Colonization Work. Cambridge: Harvard University Press, 1934.

Gentile, Frank. "Statistical Sampling--The Auditor's Best Friend." International Journal of Government Auditing, 1 (April 1974), 2-3, 16.

George, Claude S., Jr. The History of Management Thought. 2nd ed. Englewood Cliffs, NJ: Prentice-Hall, 1972.

Goetz, Billy E. Management Planning and Control. New York: McGraw-Hill, 1949.

Gordon, Robert A. Business Leadership in the Large Corporation. Washington: Brookings Institute, 1945.

Gravelle, William J. "How to Conduct an Operational Audit." Bank Administration, 50 (Sept. 1974), 76-80.

Greenwood, William T. Business Policy: A Management Audit Approach. New York: Macmillan, 1967.

Greever, William S. Arid Domain: The Santa Fe Railway and Its Western Land Grant. Stanford: Stanford University Press, 1954.

Guck, Henry H. "The Psychology of Management Audits." Management Accounting, 56 (Sept. 1974), 41-44.

Haimann, Theo, William Scott, and Patrick E. Connor. Managing the Modern Organization. 3rd ed. Boston: Houghton Mifflin, 1978.

Haines, Henry S. American Railway Management. New York: John Wiley & Sons, 1897.

Hamilton, Walton H., and Irene Till. "Property." Encyclopedia of the Social Sciences. New York: Macmillan, 1934.

Harlow, Alvin F. The Road of the Century: The Story of the New York Central. New York: Creative Age Press, 1947.

------------. Steel Ways of New England. New York: Creative Age Press, 1946.

Harvard University Research Center in Entrepreneurial History. Change and the Entrepreneur: Postulates and the Patterns for Entrepreneurial History. Cambridge, MA: Harvard University Press, 1949.

Henderson, A. M. and Talcott Parsons, trans. and eds. Max Weber: The Theory of Social and Economic Organization. New York: Free Press, 1947.

Henderson, Harold L. "Frederick Henry Harvey." Unpublished Master's Thesis, University of Kansas City, 1942.

Higgens, Neal Owen. "The Early Pension Plans of the Baltimore and Ohio and the Pennsylvania Railroads, 1880-1937." Unpublished Dissertation, University of Nebraska-Lincoln, 1974.

Hodgetts, Richard M. Management: Theory, Process, and Practice. Philadelphia: W. B. Saunders, 1975.

Hungerford, Edward. The Story of the Baltimore and Ohio Railroad. New York: G. P. Putnam's Sons, 1928.

Kast, Fremont E., and James Rosenzweig. Organization and Management. New York: McGraw-Hill, 1979.

Katz, Daniel, and Robert L. Kahn. The Social Psychology of Organizations. New York: John Wiley and Sons, 1966.

Kelly, John H. "Productivity is Something that Should be Audited." The Office, 79 (Jan. 1974), 98.

Kennedy, Charles J. Chapters on the History of the Boston and Maine Railroad System. Vol. I and Vol. 2 Part I published. Lincoln, NE: College of Business Administration, University of Nebraska-Lincoln, 1978. (Out-of-print).

Kennedy, Charles J. Comments on the History of Business and Capitalism Especially in the United States. Lincoln, NE: College of Business Administration, University of Nebraska-Lincoln, 1974.

----------. "Commuter Services in the Boston Area, 1835-1860." Business History Review, 36 (1962), 153-170.

----------. "Entrepreneurial and Managerial Appraisal in Writing Railroad History." Read at the Rocky Mountain Social Science Association, Denver, CO, April 28-29, 1972, and included in his Comments . . .

----------. Excerpts from Kennedy's Forthcoming Volumes on The History of The Boston and Maine Railroad System Selected For A Symposium on Accounting and Management Appraisal in Writing Railroad History at Denver, Colorado, April 29, 1978. Lincoln, NE: College of Business Administration, University of Nebraska-Lincoln, 1978. (Out-of-print).

----------. "Management Appraisal for Historians." Presented to a Seminar, in Economic and Business History, University of Nebraska-Lincoln, October 1971.

----------. "Measuring the Operating Efficiency of Early American Railroads." presented to a Seminar in Economics and Business History, University of Nebraska-Lincoln, 1979.

----------. New Approach to the History of the American Business System. Lincoln, NE: College of Business Administration, University of Nebraska-Lincoln, 1979.

----------. ed. Papers of the Sixteenth Business History Conference. Lincoln, NE: College of Business Administration, University of Nebraska-Lincoln, 1969.

----------. Railroad History: Entrepreneurial and Managerial Appraisal and Other Essays. To be published.

----------. Railroad Management to 1870s: The Predecessors of the Boston & Maine System. (To be published in 1981).

----------. "Top Management of American Railroads, 1830-1870." Read at the Western Social Science Association, Denver, CO, May 1, 1975.

Kerr, John L. The Louisville and Nashville: An Outline History. New York: Young and Ottley, 1933.

Kirkland, Edward C. Men, Cities, and Transportation: A Study in New England History, 1820-1900. 2 vols. Cambridge: Harvard University Press, 1948.

Klein, Maury. History of the Louisville and Nashville Railroad. New York: Macmillan, 1972.

------------. The Great Richmond Terminal: A Study in Businessmen and Business Strategy. Charlottesville: University Press of Virginia, 1970.

Knighton, Lennis M. "Information Preconditions of Performance Auditing." Governmental Finance, 5 (May 1976), 22-27.

Knuth, Oswald. Managerial Enterprise. New York: Norton, 1948.

Koontz, Harold, and Cyril O'Donnell. Management: A Systems and Contingency Analysis of Managerial Functions. 6th ed. New York: McGraw-Hill, 1976.

Krooss, Herman E., and Charles Gilbert. American Business History. Englewood Cliffs, NJ: Prentice-Hall, 1972.

Kuhn, Thomas S. The Structure of Scientific Revolutions. Chicago: University of Chicago Press, 1962.

Leonard, William P. The Management Audit. Englewood Cliffs, NJ: Prentice-Hall, 1962.

Levitt, Arthur. "The Modern Approach to Public Audits." Management Accounting, 55 (Feb. 1974), 44-46.

Luthans, Fred. Introduction to Management: A Contingency Approach. New York: McGraw-Hill, 1976.

Marshall, James. Santa Fe: The Railroad that Built an Empire. New York: Random House, 1945.

Martin, Albro. Enterprise Denied: Origins of the Decline of the American Railroads, 1897-1917. New York: Columbia University Press, 1971.

Martindell, Jackson. The Appraisal of Management: For Executives and Investors. Rev. ed. New York: Harper & Row, 1965.

McMillan, William E. "Step-wide Management Controls." Computers and People, 23 (April 1974), 8-17.

McMurry, Donald L. The Great Burlington Strike of 1888. Cambridge: Harvard University Press, 1955.

Meyer, Balthasar M. History of Transportation in the United States before 1860. Forge Village, MA: Peter Smith, 1948.

Moody, John. The Railroad Builders. New Haven: Yale University Press, 1919.

------------. How to Analyze Railroad Reports. New York: Analyses Publishing, 1912.

Mooney, James D. The Principles of Organization. New York: Harper and Brothers, 1947.

Morin, Desmond B. J. "The Operational Audit." International Journal of Government Auditing, 1 (Jan. 1974), 2-3.

Murray, Lawrence M. "Management Audit of Divisional Performance." Management Accounting, 54 (March 1973), 26-28.

Newcomb, T., and E. Hartley, eds. Readings in Social Psychology. New York: Holt, Rhinehart and Winston, 1947.

North, Douglas C. Growth and Welfare in the American Past: A New Economic History. Englewood Cliffs, NJ: Prentice-Hall, 1966.

Overton, Richard C. Burlington Route. New York: Alfred A. Knopf, 1965.

Pearson, Henry G. An American Railroad Builder: John Murray Forbes. New York: Arno, 1972.

Peterson, Wallace C. Income, Employment and Economic Growth. New York: W. W. Norton, 1967.

Pollard, Sidney. The Genesis of Modern Management, A Study of the Industrial Revolution in Great Britain. Cambridge, MA: Harvard University Press, 1965.

Poor, Henry V. Poor's Manual of the Railroads of the United States. New York, 1870-1 to 1902.

Prentice, Noble R. Southwestern Letters. Topeka, KS: Kansas Publishing House, 1882.

Research and Development Bureau of the Illinois Central Railroad. Organizational Traffic of the Illinois Central System. Chicago: Illinois Central Railroad Co., 1938.

Robertson, Ross M. History of the American Economy. 3rd ed. New York: Harcourt Brace Jovanovich, 1973.

Sagan, Carl. The Dragons of Eden. New York: Ballantine Books, 1977.

Sisk, Henry L. Management and Organization. 3rd ed. Chicago: South-Western, 1977.

Smith, Charles H., Roy A. Lanier, and Martin Taylor. "The Need and Scope of the Audit of Management: A Survey of Attitudes." Accounting Review, 47 (April 1972), 270-283.

Snellgrove, Olin C. "The Management Audit--Organizational Guidance System." Journal of Systems Management, 22 (Dec. 1971), 10.

Stevens, Frank Walker. The Beginnings of the New York Central Railroad: A History. New York: G. P. Putnam's Sons, 1926.

Stover, John F. American Railroads. Chicago: University of Chicago Press, 1961.

------------. The Railroads of the South, 1865-1900: A Study in Finance and Control. Chapel Hill: The University of North Carolina Press, 1955.

------------. History of the Illinois Central. New York: Macmillan, 1975.

Tachau, Mary K. Bonsteel. "The Making of a Railroad President: Milton Hannibal Smith and the Louisville and Nashville." Filson Club History Quarterly, XLIII (April 1969).

Taylor, Fredrick W. The Principles of Scientific Management. New York: Harper, 1911.

Taylor, George R. The Transportation Revolution, 1815-1860. New York: Harper & Row, 1951.

------------, and Irene D. Neu. The American Railroad Network 1861-1890. Cambridge: Harvard University Press, 1956.

Tersine, R. J., and M. B. Jones. "Models for Examining Organizations." Journal of Systems Management, 24 (1973), 32-37.

Thompson, J. D. Organizations in Action. New York: McGraw-Hill, 1967.

Tillett, Anthony, Thomas Kempner, and Gordon Willis. Management Thinkers. Baltimore: Penguin, 1970.

Van Gigch, J. P. Applied General Systems Theory. New York: Harper & Row, 1974.

Van Oss, S. F. American Railroads as Investments. New York: Putnam's, 1893.

Walton, Scott D. Business in American History. Columbus, OH: Grid, 1971.

Waters, L. L. Steel Trails to Santa Fe. Lawrence: University of
     Kansas Press, 1950.

Weiss, Allen. "Management Audits--The Development of a New Service."
     LKHH Accountant, 63 (Autumn 1973), 46-49.

Wixon, Rufus, ed. Accountants' Handbook. New York: Ronald Press,
     1965.

Wren, Daniel A., and Dan Voich, Jr. Principles of Management:
     Process and Behavior. 2nd ed. New York: The Ronald Press, 1976.

------------. The Evolution of Management Thought. New York: The
     Ronald Press, 1972.